A Primer for
Child Psychotherapists

A Primer for Child Psychotherapists

Diana Siskind

JASON ARONSON INC.
Northvale, New Jersey
London

Learning Resources
Centre

Production Editor: Judith D. Cohen

This book was set in 11 pt. Fairfield Light by Alpha Graphics of Pittsfield, New Hampshire and printed and bound by Book-mart Press, Inc. of North Bergen, New Jersey.

Library of Congress Cataloging-in-Publication Data

Siskind, Diana.
    A primer for child psychotherapists / by Diana Siskind.
      p. cm.
    Includes bibliographical references and index.
    ISBN 0-7657-0233-9
    1. Child psychotherapy. 2. Children—Diseases—Treatment.
    3. Child psychiatry. I. Title.
    RJ504.S543 1999
    618.92'8914—dc21   99-32689

Printed in the United States of America on acid-free paper. Jason Aronson Inc. offers books and cassettes. For information and catalog write to Jason Aronson Inc., 230 Livingston Street, Northvale, New Jersey 07647-1731. Or visit our website: http://www.aronson.com

For John, Vali, and Tony,
my best and dearest teachers

Contents

Preface

This book is a conversation with my fellow child therapists, my many colleagues who are treating children and their parents, at a time when our profession no longer offers the support systems that stood by earlier generations of child psychotherapists.

I have heard you talk about your work at seminars, have listened to your questions, and have heard you present clinical material from your large and complex caseloads. I have seen you at scientific meetings, in continuing education classes, and at training institutes, always listening, taking notes, raising your hand, seeking to expand your knowledge, and looking for guidance. I have even heard from you on the telephone, calling from remote places where seminars, supervision, and peer support are rarely available. Having nobody to consult with, you call the author of a book you read in the hope that a treatment dilemma can be addressed, more books can be recommended, and some training opportunities in your area may be discovered, always searching to grow in your ability to do your work.

There are many of you out in the field, working hard to perform your demanding jobs in agencies or in your private practices. And despite the constricting conditions imposed by our health delivery system, you often find ways to succeed because your commitment and determination override the obstacles in your way.

I've written this book for you, but I've also written it for myself because of something about the nature of our work. As you know, we've chosen a profession that requires much listening, fine tuning to the patient's communications, and always assessing the most appropriate and growth-promoting therapeutic direction. Ideally the psychotherapist speaks only to benefit the patient. Being *quiet* is an art form we develop over time in our quest to allow the patient to find his truest voice. *Writing* gives the therapist a chance to speak, to take what was silently understood during all those years of quiet listening, extract its essence, and give it shape and form . . . and words.

I hope that as you read these chapters you find answers to some of the questions you often raise, good questions that address the most basic issues in our work. I often cannot answer them with absolute specificity. Our field is too complex for that, too filled with the unknown, the unknowable, and the unexpected. But I can give you some guidelines, some principles to rest on that will not fail you once you become familiar with them. I think you will find that once you learn to use them quietly and with real understanding, they will help you to slow down, to think clearly, and to assess what is realistic and possible, what you really can do. There is great value in finding your place and your stride, and in moving at a pace most natural to the situation. And there can be much pleasure in discovering all the new questions that arise during every therapeutic encounter.

Acknowledgments

Writing books can become addictive, especially with Jason Aronson as publisher. His love of books, marvelous enthusiasm, and confident expectation go a long way toward fueling the writing momentum. And once again I've the good fortune to have Judy Cohen as my editor. I marvel at her talent for understanding what this author has set out to do, and knowing just how to fine tune and polish the final product. Thank you both very much.

Writing a third book has been a more solitary experience than that of my earlier books. Perhaps that's what happens as book writing becomes part of the normal routine of life; the process loses the sense of awe experienced while writing book one, or the nagging uncertainty about being able to do it again with book two.

Consequently the only people I asked to read my manuscript were my dear friend and colleague Beatrice Weinstein and my husband Elliott. I thank them for their continuing help and interest, and for their astute comments.

I also thank Yvonne Young for having provided me with a list of questions asked by her supervisees. Every question was used and answered to the best of my ability. I also thank my other students and supervisees who over the years have raised the questions that inspired the writing of this book. Finally I thank all my patients who helped me understand that there are no answers, only a widening circle of questions that deepen insight and make life richer and more interesting.

PART

I

On Beginning

CHAPTER

1

 ﾛ

Some Basic Differences between the Treatment of Children and the Treatment of Adults

QUESTION: What are some of the basic differences between the treatment of children and the treatment of adults?[1]

ANSWER: The differences are numerous and apply to every facet of treatment from application of theory and use of technique to the increased need for flexibility, tact, and basic common sense on the part of the therapist.

The most dramatic difference is the obvious one: the patient is a child. *The factor of youth establishes two sets of conditions of primary importance: (1) development is ongoing, and (2) the child is dependent on his parents for* basic care.

---

1. Throughout the book, questions will be printed in boldface and answers in regular type.

These conditions are at the heart of the differences between treating a child and treating an adult.[2]

QUESTION: What do you mean when you say that there is an increased need for "tact, flexibility, and basic common sense" on the part of the therapist?

ANSWER: Communication between therapist[3] and patient is fundamental to the therapeutic process and that is true whether the patient be adult or child. In our work with adults we expect that communication to be primarily verbal, but with children the verbal mode is often limited or lacking. Therefore the child therapist needs to be open to finding alternate ways of communicating with his young patients, and creative in using modes that do not rely on words alone.

Also, in treating a child[4] the therapist has ongoing contact with the child's parents. We have to fit parents into the treatment situation and find ways of communicating with them that are helpful to them *and* support the child's treatment. It is in our positioning ourselves in such a way as to be helpful to child *and* parents that tact, flexibility, and common sense come into play. Our role with parents is considered by many child therapists to be very difficult, a major stumbling block.

QUESTION: What exactly is our role with the parents of our child patients?

---

2. Italic type denotes a basic principle.

3. Psychotherapist and therapist will be used interchangeably throughout this book.

4. Throughout the book, child and children will refer to children from birth to 12 years. Adolescent and pre-adolescent will refer to children 12 and older. This dividing line, based on chronological age, is being used for the sake of expediency. We do need to recognize that emotional development does not always keep pace with chronological age.

ANSWER: *Our role with parents is to be their ally in helping them with their child.* This is where tact, flexibility, and common sense become the therapist's greatest assets.

QUESTION: Could you say a little more about why you are placing so much emphasis on the relationship with the child's parents?

ANSWER: I believe that their position in the treatment of their child has not been given due consideration. They are often seen as a hindrance to the child's treatment, and in some cases they fit that description, but perhaps they would be less likely to become a hindrance if we viewed them with more respect and concern. We need to remember that many parents experience their child's need for a therapist as a blow, an indication of their failure or shortcomings. They frequently perceive the need for treatment as meaning that something has gone wrong in their ability to care for their child, and regard their child's difficulties as their fault. Consequently they often view the therapist as someone who is going to undo the damage they did, someone who is going to do a better job with their child than they did. Imagine their shame, discomfort, and resentment at being in that position! We can be most helpful to them if we don't accept the role of "better" parent. We aren't. Our role with their child is simply different. We hope it can be shaped to have an effect complementary to theirs.

QUESTION: How do we begin our work and get on a good footing with the parents of our child patients?

ANSWER: The tone is often set when a parent first telephones us for an appointment. Obviously, it is a parent who makes that initial call. Some parents simply ask for an appointment and perhaps briefly state what precipitated the call. But in some instances the parent asks many questions about the therapist's qualifications, policies regarding the treatment of children, fees, frequency of appointments, length of time for treatment, and so forth. Some of these questions can be answered simply, others cannot. What is important here is for the therapist to accept the parent's right to ask the questions, and to view any irritation at being questioned as a signal that things are already going awry on the side of the therapist and that some self-analysis would be helpful. If we're going to establish a working alliance with the parent, and that is a high priority from the first point of contact, we have to take any irritation or annoyance we experience and transform it into information about something in the interaction that's producing such an effect in us.

QUESTION: But do you think it's appropriate for a parent to attempt an extensive telephone interview before making an appointment?

ANSWER: I prefer not to view it from the perspective of *appropriate* or *inappropriate*. More helpful to our work is to think diagnostically, to pay attention to the tone and nature of the questions. Is the tone harsh, disrespectful, suspicious? Is it anxious, tentative? What are the questions about? Might they be a simple down-to-earth attempt to get a sense of what the therapist is like before making an appointment? Or getting a sense of what to expect? If we really pay attention and listen carefully we will have a good opportunity to learn something about this referral.

QUESTION: Wouldn't it be better for the parents and for us if they asked the questions in person rather than over the phone? What if we don't have the twenty minutes they require?

ANSWER: Sure, it would be better for us if the questions were asked once they were in our consulting room, but what if these parents are too frightened to just come in? What if they need some sort of exchange with us to ease their way into our office? And if such a parent should call when we only have two minutes to spare rather than the twenty he needs, then we can tell him[5] that we will be able to talk to him in a more leisurely manner at a specific time which we name. The point is that certain parents need our help and attention to a great degree, sometimes only at the beginning stage and sometimes throughout the entire treatment process. If we accept that as one of the many conditions particular to this treatment situation and view it as an intrinsic factor that we need to understand and respect, we are much more likely to establish a working alliance with the parents.

Most therapists will accept with no ambivalence or resentment that Jaime, age 4, needs his box of miniature cars to be waiting for him on our desk when he arrives for his session. We respect the value he places on these toys and understand that he uses them in play to express himself. Yet it's so difficult for many of us to accept some of the special requirements of parents, whether it be an occasional phone call, a request that we speak to the child's teacher, that an appointment be changed, or some such expression of need that asks the therapist to extend herself in some way. We don't have to gratify all such requests, but we do have to accept them as a form of communication and try to understand them.

QUESTION: These questions have taken us in a surprising direction. When I asked about the basic difference between treating children and treating adults I never expected to focus so much on the child's parents. Now that you've convinced me that our role with them is very important, could you tell me more about starting off well with them, getting on that good footing you mentioned earlier?

---

5. Masculine and feminine pronouns will be used interchangeably throughout this book.

ANSWER: Let me give you an example of an ideal beginning.

Some time ago a woman telephoned me and said that her daughter's nursery school teacher had recommended "play therapy" for Sally who had just turned 3. The teacher had said that for quite a while now Sally seemed "out of it," and all efforts to engage her were in vain. Perhaps a child therapist would know what to do.

Sally's mother spoke in a subdued but friendly manner. I noticed that she had not mentioned her response to the teacher's referral or to Sally's state of mind. I asked whether she knew what the teacher had meant by describing Sally as being "out of it." Mrs. S. sighed and said that she understood the teacher only too well. For at least two months now Sally seemed dreamy and sad much of the day. Gone was her marvelous exuberance and the playfulness that had made her so appealing to peers and had delighted her parents and all who came in contact with her.

Mrs. S. went on to tell me that she shared the teacher's concern. Her own efforts to rekindle the lovely connection she had always had with her daughter were dismissed by the child and Sally's father fared no better. She and her husband both agreed with Sally's teacher that it was time to seek professional help. And then she asked: "But what exactly is play therapy? I've heard the term used, but I don't know what it means. Oh, this is all so new to me! The idea of my little girl needing psychotherapy is so distressing . . . and I can't imagine therapy with a child so young. I was told that you treat young children. Can you tell me how it works?"

This is what I told this worried and perplexed mother. "Young children are usually not able to express their worries and concerns verbally the way most adults can. The most natural way to approach them is through play. By providing carefully chosen toys and a welcoming atmosphere, the child therapist sets an easy and comfortable climate in which the child may begin to express herself through play. Gradually the play becomes the vehicle through which a dialogue between child and therapist develops. Through this communication the therapist gradually gains insight into the child and gets to understand the nature of the problem. Then, through the use of play, the problem gains definition and with the help of the therapist, the child begins to deal with it in a conscious way. With this in place, with the problems more distinct and understandable, the child can now communicate more effectively, not only within the therapy situation, but with everyone in her world. At that point she provides her parents with the cues they were lacking and that are essential to understanding her and providing the help and care she needs."

I told Sally's mother that with a child so young it is both useful and advisable to have one of the parents remain in the room, sometimes just as an observer and sometimes as a participant. After a period of time it may make sense to let the parent stay in the waiting room, but only if the child is comfortable enough to let the parent go. But sometimes, regardless of the child's comfort level, we decide that a tripartite situation is most productive, in which case the parent remains for the full course of treatment.

I told Sally's mother that should she decide to go ahead with the referral, she would get to see play therapy in action, but prior to seeing Sally I would want to meet with her, and preferably with Sally's father as well. We would need to discuss the current situation and get to know each other before Sally was brought to see me. I would want to know Sally's history, something about each family member, and about the family as a whole. They, the parents, would in turn get to know what I was like and would decide whether they felt comfortable about bringing their daughter to see me.

Sally's mother said it was reassuring that she and her husband would be included in the process. She asked whether I had any idea of what could cause such a dramatic change of mood in a 3-year-old child. I said rather than speculate in a general way I preferred to get to know Sally. As I got to know her and her story we would gain insight into what caused her sadness, and would then know how to go about helping her recover the good spirits that in the past had been her customary mood. An appointment with Sally's parents was made for a few days hence.

Many factors contributed to this case getting off to a good start. The mother, having fully recognized her child's sadness, and feeling very concerned about it, experienced the teacher's recommendation to seek professional help as responsible and caring. She had mentioned that her husband was also receptive to seeking help. That both parents were united in their view that a problem existed that warranted professional help was in and of itself unusual and a most fortuitous beginning.

Furthermore, Mrs. S. was forthright about her lack of knowledge about play therapy, and while the idea of treatment for so young a child was mystifying to her, she listened with interest and respect to my brief explanation. She accepted my reluctance to speculate about the cause of Sally's problem, and was willing to wait for the process to provide some answers and solutions. Everything about her tone and manner suggested that she has "confident expectation" (Benedek 1938) that help was forthcoming. This basic receptivity to human interaction colors all object relationships and goes a long way towards laying the foundation to a working alliance so essential to our work with parents (Siskind 1997).

This simple and commonplace exchange between a mother and a therapist she had never met in person, this dialogue between two strangers, one seeking help and the other offering to give it, is an example of an ideal beginning to the process of treating a child. But it also captures one of the significant differences between the treatment of adults and the treatment of children. Had the caller been an adult wishing a consultation for herself, the telephone call would typically have been brief and directed to finding an appointment time convenient to both parties. Had questions about treatment come up, they would most likely have been placed on hold until the actual appointment hour. Parents often need more help, more information, more of a sense of connection with the therapist than do adults who seek their own treatment.

It's not the style of all child therapists to have such lengthy initial telephone contacts, but in my experience I've sometimes found it a useful approach. Of course there are many times when it's not requested, and a brief telephone contact is all that's needed. There are also times when staying on the telephone with a parent we've not yet met would not be a good idea. We will get to these variations of approach and you will see that once we have some basic principles solidly behind us we will find it easier to navigate our way through the various situations that present themselves in our daily work.

2

⤲

Important Considerations in Treating Children

QUESTION: What should we think about before we begin treating a child? What are some important considerations to keep in mind?

ANSWER: Before you begin, you need to keep this important fact in mind. A child does not usually seek treatment for himself. He is brought to treatment by his parents; except for rare circumstances, treatment is imposed on him regardless of how he feels about it. As you well know, most adults seek treatment voluntarily.

Of course there are some adults whose treatment is mandated by a court of law, or who come to see a therapist under the threat of their spouse leaving them or their boss firing them or some such "or else" condition, but most adults seek the help of a psychotherapist because they are distressed with aspects of themselves or their life circumstances.

When an adult arrives in our consulting room he generally requests psychotherapy for himself, and although on occasion a prospective patient might express uncertainty about entering treatment and request a period of consultation to help determine whether treatment is appropriate, ultimately that adult makes the decision regarding his own treatment and has at least some idea that treatment is a process that involves him and the therapist talking to each other with the objective of arriving at some level of change and improvement. This is not so in regard to the child. Except for some rare circumstances the child neither seeks treatment nor understands the process ahead. These factors are of great importance and our awareness of them must become part of our general attitude towards our young patients.

QUESTION: Are you saying that the adult seeking treatment is a more motivated patient because he elected to be in treatment and knows what to expect, whereas the child is more resistant because treatment was imposed on him?

ANSWER: No. I'm not saying that at all. You reached a logical conclusion based on what I just said, but in our work the reaches of logic take unexpected turns. The adult who elected to enter treatment for himself might turn out to be a very resistant patient, whereas the child whose treatment was forced on him might become a very motivated one. We can come back to this point later.

What I had in mind in highlighting the fact that the adult's treatment is self-initiated whereas the child's is not, was to stress that very often the child does not understand why he is being brought to treatment. Consequently, what he is told about seeing a therapist is of great importance. It sets the stage for what is to become the climate of treatment, a climate that depends on the highest level of truthfulness. The child has to be told the real reason he is coming to see a therapist, and this has to be presented to him in a way appropriate to his age and stage of understanding.

QUESTION: Isn't it a very difficult undertaking to tell a child the reason he is to meet a therapist? What if the child is withdrawn and has no friends? How could one present this unhappy picture to the child without humiliating him?

ANSWER: This would indeed be very difficult if this were a social situation. We are accustomed to upholding certain standards of good manners, politeness, and restraint in discussing the person we address, especially when that person is a stranger. But when we move into our professional role some of this changes—not the politeness and good manners, that doesn't change. What changes is the quality of directness in our communications. So, no, I don't think it would necessarily be difficult to tell the child in your example the real reason for coming. We can usually assume that a withdrawn and isolated child has some awareness of his state of unhappiness. By being willing to address his predicament we are doing several things simultaneously. Our directness immediately suggests that a difference exists between us and people who act more in keeping with what is "socially correct." Because we are representing ourselves as unafraid to face things as they are, our honesty and directness could be a great relief to some children. It might hold out the hope that things can change and improve. But before we can formulate our statement to the child about the reason and purpose of his visit to our office we need to know as much as possible about him. Equally important to our ability to proceed with a measure of confidence is our having achieved a reasonably good understanding of why his parents consulted us about him.

QUESTION: Suppose Mr. and Mrs. Jones come to see you about their 8-year-old son Peter and say that he's sad and lonely and friendless and that they've been unable to help him feel better about himself. What else would you need to know in order to present the reason for the appointment and the purpose it's meant to serve?

ANSWER: I would have to know as much as possible about his infancy and early life, about his family situation, including siblings, the onset of his unhappiness, his general functioning, including his interests, something about his parents and their background and current functioning, the reason for their seeking a consultation at this time, and their attitude about treatment for their son. I would be particularly interested in having a sense of whether they viewed treatment as help or punishment or some combination of the two. For instance, if their attitude about treatment was punitive rather than hopeful, this would help me formulate an approach to them and to how their son might understand being brought to my office. This in turn would help me fine-tune my approach to his understanding of why he's been brought to see me.

QUESTION: What might you say to Peter A., son of concerned parents who want to bring their child to a therapist because they believe in treatment, have themselves been helped in the past, and are distressed that their son is suffering? What about Peter B., whose parents have negative feelings about psychotherapy but have been told by the school that they should seek the help of a therapist because of their son's general unhappiness and social isolation?

ANSWER: For me to do this, you need to accept my illustrations as being based on general principles. We do not know nearly enough about Peter A. and Peter B. to be specific in the way we present treatment to them. Every situation is unique and it's always hard to generalize, but I do recognize that it's sometimes a helpful teaching approach to give examples, so here are the illustrations you requested.

To begin with, we usually discuss *with the parents* what the child is to be told about coming to see a therapist. Often parents ask us what to tell their child and it's a good idea to turn the question back to them. You will find that many parents try to downplay the problem. Often they want to tell the child that the therapist is an acquaintance who has heard about him and would love to meet him. I find that parents have a particularly hard time being direct when their child is very young, and typically want to tell him that they're taking him to visit a friend or that he's to have a play date with a grown-up.

At this point in the discussion with the parents we can say that we've found that it works well with a child even as young as 2 or 3, to tell him the real reason for his visit. Not infrequently parents will be dismayed by this and talk about not wanting their child to feel there is something wrong with him. This then becomes a vitally important conversation to have with the parents, and chances are that they will reveal many of their own worried feelings about bringing their child for treatment. The opening up of this important subject gives the therapist many opportunities to explore, intervene, and clarify.

This dialogue is not something to rush through or to regard as being only or primarily oriented to the goal of finding the right thing to say to the child. This dialogue is also for the benefit of the parents and the therapist. It aids the therapist in understanding the parents and joining them in a spirit essential to forming a working alliance with them. The child will, of course, benefit as well, since this careful approach will lay a foundation for a level of communication between therapist and parents that will affect the child. Eventually most parents will accept the idea that telling their child the real reason for the appointment is a good way to begin, but the therapist must be flexible and accept the degree to which a particular set of parents can deal with the real reason.

For example, the parents of Peter A., who believe in treatment, might be helped to tell him, "We've noticed that you never invite friends over after school, that you spend all afternoon in your room with your computer, and that you don't look forward to doing much outside of the house. We don't understand why you want to be by yourself so much and when we try to talk to you about it you just tell us everything is fine. We aren't so sure that it's fine and we consulted a person who knows a lot about children, a child therapist. We're going to take you to see him so that you and he can figure things out together."

Now obviously, this statement could not be proposed to the parents of Peter B., since his parents do not believe in treatment and the referral was not their idea. So we have to think of what to say to their son to suit their situation and attitude and still meet the objective of giving their son an honest presentation of the situation that faces him. These parents could simply say something like this: "Your teacher and principal have noticed that you've been keeping to yourself a lot at school and that you've been very quiet in class, and they wondered whether something was bothering you. They suggested that you see a child therapist, and since they think it's a good idea we met with Mr. X. and made an appointment for you next week."

QUESTION: Are you saying that in helping the parents find an appropriate way of presenting their child with the fact that they are going to have an appointment with a therapist, we have to be as mindful of their attitude about treatment as we are of the child's initial introduction to this new experience?

ANSWER: I'm saying exactly that. *We always have to be as mindful of our communications with the parents as we are of our communications with the child.* And since there is no room for deception on any level in our work we have to keep that in mind in formulating the way the parents are to introduce their child to an appointment with us. For instance, if parents are bringing their child to us only because they were told to do so, we cannot ask them to assume an enthusiastic attitude. What remains is for them to provide a pretty straightforward account of how the referral originated. In accepting their attitude as it really is the therapist is conveying respect for their point of view.

  The child's therapist has to stand equidistant to child and parent (Siskind 1997). *Only when positioned that way can the therapist be alert to all the subtle shifts of affect and behavior that inform and guide our work.*

QUESTION: **How complicated it all sounds compared to the treatment of adults! Every time I ask a question about the child we end up talking about the parent. Is the parent always looking over our shoulder?**

ANSWER: I wouldn't put it quite that way. I would rather say that the parent is always there as an essential factor in the child's treatment. A parent is present in the child's life in two ways. There's the real parent and his vital role in the child's life and development, and there's the child's intrapsychic representation of that parent. In other words, the child has his own growing and changing perceptions of that parent. Our job is to know, as best we can, the real parent, learn to understand the child's version and experience of that parent, and also view the parent as becoming the recipient of our help and attention.

  If we view the parent as looking over our shoulder we're in trouble. That expression has such obvious superego im-

plications that we would have to wonder whether we have converted that parent into a parental presence in our own past, a
common form of countertransference in child treatment.

QUESTION: Once we've found a way for the parents to
present the appointment with a therapist to their child,
how do we follow this up when we see the child?

ANSWER: It's a natural way to start. It gives us the opportunity
to define our function right at the beginning. In a typical
situation we would greet the parent and child in the waiting
room, introduce ourselves to the child, or let the parent introduce us if they seem so inclined. If the child is young,
say 8 or younger, we would invite them both into the office,
or we might ask the child whether she would prefer her
parent in the room with us or in the waiting room. If the child
is older we would invite just the child into the office and
tell her that her parent will stay in the waiting room. If the
child looked unhappy about separating from the parent we
would ask whether she wanted her parent to join us.

I chose age 8 as a dividing point between young and not
so young. This is a pretty arbitrary demarcation. You have to
use your judgment based on your knowledge of the child as
provided by the parents and by the child's affect and general demeanor when you first see her. If the parent's inclu-
sion in the room has been discussed and agreed upon prior
to the appointment, you can stick to that plan.

QUESTION: Is our goal to see the child alone as soon as the
child is comfortable with that arrangement?

ANSWER: No, not at all. I'll tell you why I feel strongly about
this in a minute, but let me say that many therapists disagree with me and have as their goal getting the parent out
of the consulting room as fast as possible, no matter what
the circumstances or the stage of treatment.

My thinking is as follows. Let's remember that we're presently discussing the consultation period, not treatment proper. Let's say that we've been told by the parents why they've contacted us. Now we need to fill out the story by observing the child and the interaction between the child and the parents. We need to understand what's going on, whether anything has gone askew, and where our interventions need to be aimed. Just because the parents have requested treatment for their child doesn't necessarily mean that that would be the best route to take. *We need to understand what needs to be treated!* Seeing the child with one of his parents gives us valuable insight into the situation.

While it's true that some children might feel freer to talk if there is no parent in the room, this kind of information is in itself very important to our understanding of the total picture and it will emerge in good time. Let me go on with what might actually happen during that initial visit with the child and how you might introduce her to the reason she's come to see you.

Once the child is in your office, if she's talkative, friendly, and interested in exploring your office, you go along with her wish to see what the place is like, and, in the process, what the therapist is like. If the child is shy, constricted, and unable to find a comfortable place for herself, you might verbalize the unfamiliarity of your room and help her find a comfortable place or activity. You behave hospitably following the good advice of Ella Freeman Sharpe (1930), who recommends that we treat our patients with the tact and courtesy we would extend to a guest.

Then, when the child has settled in, you ask whether she knows why she's come to see you. If she says she doesn't know, that doesn't mean she hasn't been told. Often a child will claim not knowing and the parent who brought her will gently, or indignantly, or matter-of-factly remind her that she was told such and such. Or the child might tell you something very different from what had been planned by you and the parents, as for instance: *"My mommy told me that you're her friend and that you don't have any children of your own so you wanted to play with me."* Well, if something like that comes out the parent might become embarrassed, defensive, or amused.

The point is not so much what the child tells you or doesn't tell you. The point is that you are able to observe so much in those first few minutes, and, based on your observations, can pick the moment when you will define the problem area in her life as presented by her parents and introduce your role with her.

QUESTION: But suppose the child tells you she was told that it was a play date with a grown-up. Suppose the child is 5. How would you know whether she was really told that by her parents or whether she was making it up on the spot? Isn't this a very tricky situation, what with the parent in the room watching you and maybe being very embarrassed?

ANSWER: Your question contained all the answers. I might not know whether she was making up a story if she sounded fairly serious and her mother remained silent. But if she said it with a big grin and her mother was amused and commented that Jane loved making up stories, then I might believe she was pulling my leg. In either event I could comfortably say that it *was* a kind of play date with a grown-up, but it would be a special kind of play date because I was a special kind of grown-up. I might pause at that point and ask Jane whether she knew what kind of grown-up I was. If greeted with silence I might say that since she didn't answer me I didn't know whether that was a "yes" or a "no" so I would go on and tell her because I wanted her to know what kind of grown-up I was. Then I might say something like, "I'm a grown-up who helps children and parents . . . I'm a special kind of helper." Then I might say something about what I was told she might need help with, or I might wait a while and let her play or seek out her mother or do whatever she chose to do. I would wait if I sensed that what I had said so far needed to be digested for a bit.

QUESTION: I know this is a hard question to answer, but could you give me some case scenarios of how a particular response in this 5-year-old child might shape your next response?

ANSWER: It's not really so hard if we remember that we have a mission. We want to introduce the child to a new situation unlike anything she's ever experienced. I'm assuming that she's never before been in the office of a therapist. And we want her mother or father, whichever one brought her, to be present during this exchange.

All right. Suppose Jane was quiet for a bit and then walked over to my couch and asked, "Is this where you sleep?" Her question would tell us that she was curious about me, the therapist, and the entire situation she found herself in. I would take her interest as a signal that she was ready to hear more. I would then tell her that I didn't sleep on that couch and that this was not my home, it was my office. I would then mention that being in this place with a special kind of grown-up was a new experience for her and something she wasn't used to. So I would tell her why she was here and then she could play or ask me questions or do anything she wished. I would then proceed to tell her what her parents and I had agreed on about the purpose of her visit.

QUESTION: And if after telling her that you were a special kind of grown-up she walked over to her mother and said, "Mommy let's go home" or just climbed into her mother's lap and started to suck her thumb, what would you do then?

ANSWER: If she asked her mother to take her home I would let her mother handle it. If I saw that her mother couldn't do it I might say that one of the special things about coming to see me is that we always have forty-five minutes together and then we say goodbye, and so far we hadn't used up our time. Perhaps we could figure out how to spend the rest of our time in a way that would make her want to stay.

If Jane got very upset I might ask her mother how she helped Jane get over her upsets; then I would fade into the background and observe and let her mother take over.

My objective is twofold: (1) to learn as much as I can about this child, the parent who brings her, and their interaction and (2) to present myself and the therapy situation as something new and useful to both of them.

If Jane climbs into her mother's lap and sucks her thumb my objective doesn't change; I still observe and interact in the particular way that defines my role and purpose. I might, for instance, say something like: "When you're in a new place with a person you don't know and you suddenly don't like it, you remember that you have your mommy's lap to climb into."

What I'm trying to convey to you is the following. *When we are able to maintain our professional attitude, then no matter what develops, no matter what's tossed our way, we catch it and we make constructive use of it. We have no agenda for the content that's presented to us. Our goal is to use whatever happens during each session in a way that defines and shapes the treatment process, and, of course, builds a working alliance with child and parents.*

3

༐

The Presenting Problem

QUESTION: What are some of the common reasons that prompt a referral to a child therapist?

ANSWER: Childhood fears constitute a large category of referrals. There are fears of going to sleep, of being alone, of going to school, of any change of routine, of the toilet, of baths, the elevator, strangers, and so forth.

Then there are social problems. Some children are unable to find a place for themselves in the world of peers and live in social isolation. There are problems around impulse control, such as children who bully others and are feared, unable to regulate their behavior, and easily out of control. There are children whose development is very uneven, advanced beyond their years in some areas and lagging behind in others. Often these children with uneven development have difficulties with peers and social situations.

There are children who do not exhibit a particular symptom picture but have been exposed to adverse conditions and are considered at risk, and there are those who've been seriously abused or traumatized and are having trouble learning, concentrating, sleeping, getting along with others, and so forth. There are children who are depressed, withdrawn, or hyperactive.

I have named some of the symptoms and situations that precipitate the referrals of children. They constitute what is known as *the presenting problem*, the factor named as the reason for contacting a child therapist. Despite the fact that this factor might have been in existence for years it is now being offered as the reason a consultation is being sought. During the initial interview it is generally useful to ask the parents what made them decide to seek the opinion of a professional at this time. But this question has to be asked tactfully, lest the parents feel criticized by what they might experience as the implication that they waited too long, not long enough, or whatever fits the nature of their anxieties.

As we listen carefully to what the parents have to say during that initial appointment, we try to learn what these symptoms might represent in the psychic development of this particular child. So many different types of situations emerge. For instance, sometimes the parents describe a child who has always been demanding, stubborn, and extremely controlling. We then learn that the parents have always been extraordinarily willing to yield to the demands of their child but when that child began school and entered a new world, the one outside the home, she was suddenly expected to be flexible and willing to conform to the structure of school and peers. The contrast between home and school was a shock and caused all sorts of difficulties, which prompted the call to a therapist.

What I just described is a very different situation than one in which something within the child changed. For instance, the sudden appearance of intense fears in a child who had appeared generally comfortable with his world would lead us to a different path of questioning and exploring.

The same care in listening would, of course, apply in the case of children whose referral is not precipitated by any behavior on the part of the child, but rather from the recognition that this child has been exposed to extraordinary events or difficult environmental conditions. Since we know that extreme events and conditions are bound to take their toll, we would be interested in the absence of apparent reaction in some children and what that could signify in terms of their development.

QUESTION: How would you go about tracing a symptom to its cause, or exploring the lack of reaction to extreme events or a malignant environment?

ANSWER: That is a very delicate task requiring a dual focus. One line of information is the result of what we learn in taking a history of the child. Here, in talking to the parents, we would need to carefully elicit a thorough picture of the child in order to become acquainted with her temperament and character style.

The second part of our information-gathering process is the result of our direct contact with the child and what we learn from our observations of and exchange with our young patient. Then we would have the intriguing task of considering whether our picture of the child meshed with that of her parents.

Of course what I'm describing is a pretty standard approach to any evaluation. However, in situations in which the child is not exhibiting any visible signs of stress we might feel our sense of direction is less clear. We might feel we have less to offer the child who does not appear to be suffering. Or we might be concerned that our appearance on the scene might upset the child's equilibrium, which the child might be desperately guarding. All in all we are more in the dark in these situations, therefore all the more in need of finding out as much as we can before coming to any conclusions or making any recommendations.

QUESTION: What about going beyond the parents and child in our information-gathering process? When are ancillary contacts appropriate?

ANSWER: In some cases our evaluation includes interviews or telephone contact with other significant people in the life of the child. Sometimes a telephone contact with the teacher is warranted. Sometimes, in the case of two working parents, an interview with the child's caregiver is useful. If medical problems play a part in the child's situation the therapist needs to understand them and might need to talk to the child's doctor.

There are children who present a very confusing diagnostic picture so that sometimes it's difficult to decide whether we're dealing with neurological problems, severe ego deficits, or a psychotic structure. When faced with diagnostic dilemmas we have the option of getting help from our colleagues in neurology and requesting a consultation. Or, when appropriate, we request psychological tests in the hope of clearing up diagnostically puzzling situations.

There are also situations wherein the referral to us was precipitated by psychological tests. When that's the case, we would want to see the report and most likely want to have a talk with the psychologist, particularly since reports are now written with the knowledge that parents will receive a copy. In the past, parents were not given copies of psychological reports and although that had disadvantages, the current system has some as well. Reports that are written with parents in mind are watered down to make them more comprehensible to lay people, and also are slanted to avoid upsetting the parents too much. The child's thoughts and fantasies might not be included in order to spare the parents from finding their content alarming. Consequently it's usually advisable to speak to the psychologist and perhaps look at the raw data if it's available.

There are situations we encounter that might prompt us to seek a psychiatric evaluation. We might make such a request if the child we're evaluating is currently taking medication for an emotional condition and we have some question about the advisability of this course of treatment. Or, we might feel that a child we've evaluated is so severely depressed or anxious or agitated that we might want to explore the usefulness of medication for him. Or, we might find that the child being evaluated is in need of hospitalization and we need a psychiatrist to bring this about.

Of course any referrals to allied professionals and all ancillary contacts should take place after discussions with the parents and with their written release. Also, the therapist should carefully consider the real need for and timing of such contacts. Sometimes we become too eager to just gather as much information as possible. Sometimes we do that because we're confused by the picture presented to us. Gathering additional factual information often does not help our state of confusion. In some cases, our state of confusion is as valuable a source of information as we can get, for it reflects something about the climate of the family we are trying to get to know.

So in short, by all means make use of ancillary contacts to fill gaps of information, but before you set out to do this, ask yourself whether it's really in the best interest of the case to proceed in this way.

QUESTION: What are some of the questions we ask parents that give us valuable information about the child's temperament?

ANSWER: They begin early in the evaluation process when we take a history of the child's early development and interweave the factual with the affective and characterological aspects of development. We want to know about the pregnancy, the delivery, the birth weight, the Apgar score, and anything else the parents want to tell us about the early stage of their child's life. But equally important will be finding out what kind of a baby he was: calm, fretful, easy to soothe, able to mold when held, inconsolable, and so forth. We will want to know about eating patterns: breast or bottle feeding, digestive difficulties, acceptance of new foods, predictability in patterns of eating and sleeping, and so forth. We will, of course, be interested in a first smile, cooing and babbling, periods of alertness, thumb sucking, and general mood.

We will ask about the baby's response to routines: baths, dressing, diaper changing. As we move along we will want to know something about stranger anxiety at around eight months, and caretaking arrangements regarding primary and other caregivers. We will ask about the common landmarks of talking, walking, weaning, eating solid foods, and such. We'll expand on this subject in the next chapter, which will deal specifically with the evaluation process.

In listening to the information the parents give us we will ask ourselves whether this was a baby who patterned well and enjoyed his food and the human interaction that went with it. Was this a smiling, robust baby who was easily satisfied, who gave his caregivers pleasure at meeting his needs? Was this a fretful and easily frustrated infant, difficult to comfort, difficult to soothe, not likely to make his caregivers feel competent and effective? Was this an ambitious baby who tried to master the next landmark before being quite ready, always working, trying, pushing? Or was this a passive baby who didn't strain but waited until the execution of the next developmental feat was relatively effortless?

We are interested in learning about early landmarks to see whether they fall within the average and ordinary time frame of early childhood. But even more important is the information we gain about this baby's temperament from the beginning, and the effect of this particular baby in interaction with the temperaments of his parents. Some parents feel more comfortable with a passive baby, some with a spunky one, and some have a gift for accepting whatever kind of baby comes their way and adapting to his needs and style.

QUESTION: How does it help us work with a child who is fearful if we know that ever since he was little he was afraid of change and wasn't venturesome?

ANSWER: We would know we were dealing with a pattern of behavior that was consistent from the beginning of his life. At the same time we would have gotten to know his parents well enough to have a sense of how their child's fearfulness affected them. For some parents, a fearful child is simply a child who needs extra protection, for others he might be experienced as a disappointment, and for others still, he might seem a narcissistic blow. This last group of parents might not be able to offer the atmosphere of safety so necessary to a child whose ego endowment renders him unable to handle the ordinary vicissitudes of life. We have to keep in mind that for some young children, a haircut or a trip to the shoe store or to the supermarket can be upsetting to the point of being traumatic.

    Some parents have a hard time accepting their child's temperament if it does not meet their fantasy of an ideal child. They might try to force a child into a role that does not fit, further exacerbating an ongoing problem. Some children who are afraid of dogs are forced to pet every dog on the street in order to master the fear, or if the child fears social situations, he is sent to after-school classes and weekend group activities in order that he may "grow out of it." These turn out to be nothing more than repeated experiences of suffering and failure. In ascertaining that a fearful child has an environment unattuned to his need for help in feeling safe, we would already have an important clue as to how to proceed.

QUESTION: How, then, would you proceed with a fearful child whose parents were unattuned to his special needs?

ANSWER: In working with this child, it would be important to help him identify the affective state he's been living in. I might, for instance, tell him that too much of the time he has not felt safe and comfortable, and that's why he was in my office today. That he and I were going to work hard together and get to understand why it is that way, and then work hard together to change the situation.

   With the parents of this child there would be a complementary goal of presenting them with a picture of their child that might be more acceptable than the one they had formed. This is, of course, very tricky and it would depend a lot on how receptive either or both of them were to gaining a different perspective of their child.

QUESTION: What could you possibly say to parents who are disappointed in their child to make them more accepting? It seems a tall order.

ANSWER: It is, but that's all right. There are a lot of tall orders in our work. Sometimes a very slight shift in attitude is the beginning of major changes. For instance, what might bring about such a shift of attitude might be the way the therapist talks to the parents about their child. She might describe something about his fearfulness and his effort to conquer it, and the special courage a fearful child need muster to do those ordinary things that other children do with little thought and effort. The experience of hearing what the therapist has to say, and noting in her tone of voice the respect she feels for the child's predicament and for his struggle, and the empathy she conveys for the child and his parents could be one of those mutative factors that begins the course of change. Please keep in mind that parents who are disappointed in their child are suffering too. Perhaps their child represents some shameful self-representation, or perhaps the child is experienced as punishment for their badness, an exposure of their shortcomings. Whatever the fantasy, the appearance of this new person, this stranger, the therapist, causes a shift. And no matter how imperceptible this shift might seem, or how skeptical their attitude that any change is possible, let us assume, on faith alone if there is no other visible indicator, that the fact of their being in our office holds a kernel of hope that things could improve. Why else did they come?

QUESTION: Some parents have no choice. They've been forced to come under the threat that their child will be expelled from school, placed in foster care, or some such dire consequence.

ANSWER: True, and some parents are unable to care or feel invested even under these dire circumstances, while others mobilize themselves and take a step in a constructive direction. We will discuss these extreme situations later.

Right now I would like to emphasize an attitude on the part of the therapist that is the most constructive position to take. *It is essential that the therapist view a parent's voluntary appearance in the consulting room as signifying that that parent has a degree of hope that matters could change, a belief, no matter how slight, that help exists and is possible. Sometimes the therapist can do little else than represent that hope.* This is particularly true at the beginning of an evaluation, before the therapist has a good grasp of the situation, or in an unusually difficult situation.

We know that our work has the potential of bringing about permanent change. Not everyone knows that as we do. I would speculate that if a therapist feels no hope at all in regard to a particular situation, it is either an indication that countertransferential forces are at play, or that the case indeed contains some particularly malignant pathology.

But let me return to the child who is experienced by his parents as a disappointment, and who experiences himself in kind, as a disappointing child. Chances are that he is not going to become a disappointing patient, because when we see him trying to play that role with us we will be very much engaged by this enactment and it will keep us well occupied. We will find it pretty interesting to work with this child who places himself in the masochistic role of being a disappointment to his *therapist*.

Remember, we therapists talk about these things. With us, they do not go leaden, unidentified; we don't allow them to become silently toxic. We take hold, we put words to them. We make good use of all communications, no matter how oblique or insidious or hard to identify. This attention to the unstated and interest in the ambiguous is one of our special attributes.

QUESTION: So what about the "presenting problem"? Would you say it's just the outward manifestation of a much bigger condition?

ANSWER: Yes, but take out the word "just." We don't want to treat the presenting problem with disrespect. It brought this family into our office. It served that purpose by being acceptable enough and unacceptable enough at the same time. It's what this family can deal with at the present moment. We don't want to convey that a much bigger and deeper problem is the "real" issue. The presenting problem is what we are handed and that's where we begin our work of exploring.

4

The Evaluation Process

QUESTION: Could you describe the objectives of an evaluation process? Is it the same in the treatment of children as it is in the treatment of adults?

ANSWER: The answer is yes and no. Let me explain. *The objective of an evaluation is to have an understanding of the person we are treating so that our treatment plan and therapeutic interventions fit the diagnostic picture of the actual patient before us.*

For example, in our treatment of adult patients, we would work one way with a patient who, because of his psychotic structure, has great difficulty in handling the most ordinary day-to-day situations; we would work quite differently with a high-functioning neurotic patient, whose area of conflict is, for example, manifested by difficulties in his love life, but who is able to do well in his work and in activities that don't involve intimate relationships.

I picked patients at opposite extremes of the diagnostic spectrum to convey how deeply our technique is shaped by our understanding of the patient. The need for diagnostic clarity as a requisite and vital factor for formulating our treatment approach is basic to all of our work, equally true with adults and children. This is the part of my answer to your question that gets a "yes"; the objectives of the evaluation period are the same for children and for adults. That's the simple part. Now comes the complicated part.

In the case of an adult who consults us about himself we know who the patient is, for there he is, sitting in our office and telling us his story. This is not so simple when parents consult us about their child.

Sometimes parents come about their child but it turns out, if we take our time and don't rush in before having explored the situation, that they have come about their marriage. Or sometimes they come about their child and it turns out that the mother is depressed and is not able to ask for help for herself but can ask on behalf of another, such as her child. And sometimes it is indeed the child who needs to be in treatment.

QUESTION: Are you saying that in child treatment, one of the purposes of an evaluation is to determine who the patient is, the child or the parent?

ANSWER: Yes. *The purpose of an evaluation is not only to assess strength and pathology. It's also a process of taking stock of the need for treatment, the readiness for treatment, and how to begin.* That, ideally, is what an evaluation should determine. *When an evaluation pertains to a child, we have to thoroughly assess the child and the parents and only then decide who the patient should be, who would most benefit from treatment at this time.* But that's just the beginning, and it's not an either/or situation. Sometimes it's the child, or the parent, or both, and/or the marital relationship. When a situation re-

quiring treatment for several family members arises, my
approach is to refer the various family members to appropriate therapists. There are, as you know, family therapists
who would work with all the family members as a group, but
that is not a treatment modality that I practice. Still, I
thought I should mention it as something that's done by those
trained to work that way.

QUESTION: Wouldn't the parents be overwhelmed to suddenly be faced with a string of referrals?

ANSWER: Absolutely. Therefore we would not make them all
at once, and chances are that we would not have a clear idea
of what is needed until we had gotten to know more about
the people and the situation. We would begin in the most
logical and acceptable place, let the case evolve, and make
additional recommendations as it moved along and with it
our growing understanding of the entire situation.

But let me go on. There's another important difference
between the evaluation of a child and that of an adult. In
adult treatment we gather the information we need directly
from the patient in order to make our diagnosis. We do this
in a leisurely way.[6] Our approach is not directive; we don't
ask specific questions of the patient but rather allow her to
tell her story in her own way and in the order she chooses.
We are as interested in contiguity as in content, in what is
provided and in what is omitted.

This is not so in child treatment. As mentioned earlier,
here we need the parents to provide most of the informa-

---

6. I am differentiating the diagnostic assessment of a patient
voluntarily seeking treatment from the standard psychiatric interview
utilized for a quick assessment of mental status in the case of patients
being admitted to psychiatric hospitals or found in various emergency
situations.

tion and we do have a general agenda. We want to know the child's history from the very beginning. We want to know whether this child's birth was planned, how the pregnancy and delivery went, how he ate and slept and behaved during earliest infancy. We're interested in early landmarks: smiling, cooing, his response to being held, to changes of routine, to change of caretakers and so forth. We are looking for basic information about his ego endowment: his ego's ability to adapt to both inner and outer stress, to pleasure, to stimulation, and so forth. We want to know whether his current difficulties represent a change or a continuation of patterns that existed from birth.

There's more involved in this line of inquiry. As we talk to the parents and explore their child's early history, we learn a great deal about *them*. We learn about their experience of parenthood and how it affected them individually and vis-à-vis each other. We learn about the object environment they created for their child, the emotional climate of his early life. We learn this from the way our questions are answered, from what is remembered and what is forgotten, from the affects they express as they revisit their child's arrival into their lives and the days that followed, from the impact of his presence on their lives, on their relationship, and on their family.

So you see, it's a big task we take on as we embark on the evaluation process in child treatment. But when we go about it in a thorough way we do get to identify the primary patient, or patients. Now what is particularly different here from the treatment of adults is that we depend on the parents to provide us with much of the information necessary for forming a diagnosis of the child, which will be supplemented by our own observations once we meet the child. At that point we will be able to round out the picture, including our impressions of his current state, his vulnerabilities, and his strengths. But in the process of providing all this information about the child, the parents reveal a great deal about themselves.

QUESTION: Could you say a little more about reaching a diagnostic understanding of the child? You seem to go way beyond the kind of information listed in the *DSM-IV* manual.

ANSWER: You're right. I'm talking about a descriptive developmental diagnosis (Blanck and Blanck 1974) that's very different from the *DSM-IV* concept of diagnosis. In the *DSM-IV* system you are basically following a list of symptoms that form a cluster of features that are given a name. This name is then placed on insurance forms with some assurance of uniformity in its usage. It doesn't inform, it doesn't enlighten, it simply categorizes.

A descriptive developmental diagnosis is quite a different matter. It begins with birth and traces the various developmental lines: psychosexual development, drive taming processes, object relations, adaptive functioning, anxiety level, defensive function, identity formation, and processes of internalization (Blanck and Blanck 1974). It maps out the changes that takes place on all these interrelated developmental lines when growth is unhampered by internal and external obstacles. It also allows us to note and chart uneven patterns of development when less than optimal conditions have prevailed. When I talk of less than optimal conditions I refer not only to environmental conditions imposed by extreme poverty, or to the type of neglect that can result from parental pathology. I include as well such constitutional factors as might seriously burden development, such as blindness, deafness, serious medical conditions, and other circumstances beyond anyone's control such as the serious illness of other family members, accidents, natural disasters, and other instances of extraordinary bad luck.

QUESTION: Would you give a clinical example that would illustrate how you combine all the pieces that need to be considered in the evaluation of a child case?

ANSWER: Mr. and Mrs. Green consult you about their son Rick, who is 10, fat, physically clumsy, and blushes easily. These characteristics have gained him a scapegoat position at school where he is repeatedly teased by his classmates and blushes in response, further intensifying his lack of status with his peers and making his day at school a dreaded event. Rick's teachers have talked to him and have tried to be supportive. His gym teacher has spent extra time coaching him in an effort to improve his coordination. A neurological examination has revealed that there is nothing neurologically wrong, but that his awkwardness is the result of lack of confidence compounded by his excess weight. His parents have discussed the problem with him and have tried to limit his intake of fattening foods. Rick himself is miserable about his inadequacies but believes that nothing can help him. Finally the school psychologist makes the referral for treatment and the parents arrive in your office and describe this situation to you.

In the course of the consultation you notice that the father talks about his wish that Rick develop some "grit" and shed these "girlish" ways lest he be tagged a "sissy" for life. The father says that his efforts to make a "man" of him are all in vain. He goes on to say that his wife feels too sorry for Rick and he fears that her indulgence of his "weakness" is detrimental to his growth. They don't see eye to eye on matters.

While he talks you are aware of his frustration and you also note his tone of contempt for his son and his wife.

Now the mother talks and cries while she talks. Rick was always a sensitive child, more interested in books and puzzles and his computer than in sports and rough and tumble games. His father wanted a different kind of a boy to be his son and was never open to getting to know the son he had. She feels that the father's disappointment was palpable from early in Rick's life. She thinks Rick is the way he is because he senses that he's a disappointment to his father, and every time he experiences another failure he feels shame and confirmation of his worthlessness. She can understand how painful that must be because she feels that she too is a disappointment to her husband, a very disappointing wife.

The therapist listens and notes beneath her humble tone the sadness, seething anger, and devastating hurt.

Based on what you've heard so far, who is the patient and what needs to be treated?

QUESTION: The case of Rick begins with a straightforward referral request: a 10-year-old boy who is fat, clumsy, blushes very easily, and becomes the class scapegoat because of it. But then we discover in the first interview with the parents that they are deeply angry at each other and each considers the other responsible for the boy's problem. You've certainly made your point in conveying how complicated it gets, and yet this example seems very much within the normal range of referrals . . . there's nothing exotic about it. How do you go about sorting out where to begin?

ANSWER: I would want to know how each of the parents feels about the idea of Rick being in treatment. Has either of them any experience with therapy, either personally or through other family members? Do they think Rick would take to the idea? Do they have any questions to ask me about how I work and how we would proceed?

If they seemed disposed to pursuing treatment for Rick I would outline the evaluation process as consisting of my seeing them separately and together to gather information about Rick and something about them, their other children, and family life in their home. At some point in this process I would meet Rick once or twice or more, to get a sense of how he feels about treatment. Then I would meet with the parents again and share my findings and recommendations.

I might tell them, if they seemed generally receptive, that the weight, clumsiness, and blushing could be viewed as symptoms, an outer manifestation of something within Rick that he can't express any other way. I might say that unfortunately, these particular symptoms are causing him a lot of distress in terms of shame and loss of self-esteem. Also, his problems are robbing him of the pleasures of good peer relations, so important at this age. I might also tell them that however unfortunate the effect of his symptoms is in terms of his daily life, the fact that they are so disruptive also has a good side. It's a loud and clear signal that help is indicated. Sometimes a symptom is so quiet and unobtrusive that it fails to be noted and the problem is allowed to go unattended.

I would probably conclude by telling the parents that we must find the best approach to helping Rick deal with what's happening to him.

QUESTION: I notice that you give the parents a general idea of how the evaluation process will proceed, but you remain tentative about whether the child will actually enter treatment. If I were the parents I would ask you why you sound tentative about Rick entering treatment. How would you answer?

ANSWER: I would tell the parents that entering treatment is a big commitment for them and for Rick. My job at present is to make sure that the decision to proceed with Rick entering treatment at this time in his life was well thought out.

For instance, if either parent had serious reservations about this course of action, it would be better to explore them and hopefully resolve the matter before Rick became invested in the process of treatment. We wouldn't want him to be invested in a process that brought him parental disapproval.

That's as much as I would say to the parents about that aspect, but I want to say more to you about it because this cannot be stressed enough. Suppose Rick found therapy not only helpful insofar as he could at last talk freely about his situation, but also because it offered him the hope that change was possible, that he wouldn't have to live his life in such misery. Imagine the enormity of the treatment situation for a boy who had been so isolated, and then imagine his intense disappointment and conflict were his interest in his treatment to bring him parental disapproval or have some such negative cast.

Finally, I would tell these parents it was very important that they work with a therapist who seems competent and trustworthy to them; they should take their time considering this factor. Nobody can predict how long treatment will last and the spirit of collaboration between therapist and parents is an important safeguard to keeping the therapeutic journey on a good course.

QUESTION: Is it always important to impress upon the parents that their participation is so central to the treatment process?

ANSWER: More often than not their role is very important, particularly if the child is young. But there are exceptions. If you sense that one or both parents are strongly anti-treatment but might agree to send a child because they've been given an ultimatum by the school and have no choice, it would be counterproductive to stress the need for their participation. Then the therapist might have to consider whether she was willing to take on a case that began with such a limitation. There are certainly cases where a lot of good work could be done without the parents' participation, and the way a case seems at the beginning and how it might change a year or so later is an unknown factor. A parent who is very anti-treatment might have a shift in attitude upon seeing considerable growth in her child and experiencing a consistently respectful attitude on the part of the therapist.

On the other hand, these exemplary conditions could also bring no change of attitude in a "nonbelieving" parent, and the child's improved state could be dismissed as the effect of normal maturation and not in the least related to the therapeutic work.

QUESTION: Could we go on with Rick a while longer and consider several scenarios and how you might deal with each?

ANSWER: Yes, but please remember that we're playing, we're making up situations, and we're doing it for learning purposes. It's not a bad learning tool but it's different from dealing with specific people and situations. Why don't you invent some of the possible ways the case of Rick might go and I'll respond.

QUESTION: Let's say at the end of the evaluation you've decided that Rick should begin therapy, and when you tell the parents, they're split on the idea of treatment for him. The father is against treatment and the mother is for it. What would you do?

ANSWER: I would tell them that treatment requires certain conditions in order to be effective. It's always preferable for the parents to be in favor of it, but if one or both parents are not, then we have to explore that situation and find out whether it is reason *not* to proceed. I would ask the father whether he would be willing to meet with me alone once or several times and explore his objections to treatment for Rick.

QUESTION: What if he refuses to meet with you to even discuss treatment?

ANSWER: Then I would ask whether he would be willing to meet with me and his wife to discuss it. And if he refused to do that I would ask him whether he was unwilling to have Rick see a therapist or just skeptical that such a process had merit. You see, at that point in the evaluation process I would have quite a bit of information about Mr. G. I would have met with him several times, probably mainly with his wife but most likely alone as well, and I would have met with Rick once or twice. In other words, this father would have cooperated in the evaluation process up to this point. This would not fit with the picture of a man completely unwilling to have his child receive help. I would want to know what Mr. G. would like to do at this point. Perhaps he envisages another approach. Perhaps he would say that rather than have me see Rick he would prefer for me to work with his wife, to try to help her stop infantilizing their son. Or perhaps he would say he needed to know more of what went on in treatment before agreeing to let his son begin.

There are so many possible objections that a parent might have about placing a child in therapy, and while some of them might be presented in the most cogent way, often the real reason is not really known to the parent but rather experienced as a disquieting anxiety that has origins beyond any conscious grasp.

It's hard to predict what might emerge from meetings with a parent who does not feel ready to allow his child to be in treatment.

QUESTION: So what do we do? The child needs treatment and one parent says "okay" and the other says "not okay." What do we do? Do we allow the no-saying parent to win out?

ANSWER: Listen to how upset you sound! There is important information in your upset state. What does it tell you?

QUESTION: It tells me that I think it's a shame that a 10-year-old boy who needs treatment and has a terrible time without it is at the mercy of a father whose pride or ignorance causes him to reject it, and that a caring mother who wants her son to be helped is too weak to deal with her bully husband's ignorance. What does a therapist do with this kind of stalemate?

ANSWER: I understand your frustration, but you're falling into a dangerous position, and it's that most common pitfall of child therapy: you're overidentified with the child. Look at the effect of that. You're mad at the father for being too powerful and mad at the mother for being too weak. You've lost your professional footing and are unable to maintain that necessary stance of listening, noting, and understanding. You are not standing equidistant between child and parents, but all the way over in the child's corner. You are in serious trouble with this case.

Look, the most important message that the therapist can convey in a situation like this is that she has made certain recommendations based on her understanding of the total situation. Whether the parents accept these recommendations or don't is up to them.

I know you don't like the idea that Rick might go without help, and I don't like it either, but most critical at this juncture is not to convey to these parents that your investment in his future is purer, deeper, and stronger than theirs. Remember, these parents consulted you for your professional opinion. They have not offered to hand their child over to you. Consider that carefully. It's really important.

QUESTION: That's all well and good, but what if these parents just walk away and Rick continues to struggle without help?

ANSWER: That's possible. But remember that they have, all three of them, been through the evaluation process. They have had a taste of dealing with a respectful professional person who conducted herself with concern for all three of them, who asked intelligent questions, made meaningful comments, and revealed a way of thinking and of processing information that many people would find quite different from what they're accustomed to. For instance, the parents have been told that the overeating, clumsiness, and blushing are symptoms, that something is going on in their child that he can only express in this way. This is probably different from their view of the matter; they probably thought that what we consider to be the symptoms are the problem. Furthermore, the problem has been acknowledged and defined for all of them. That in itself is an important shift in the family dynamics. Don't be so sure that the father is going to veto the whole thing. He might come around. Or he might not do so now but be back in a month, after the school calls him in to urge him to move on this, or his wife finds the strength to sway him, or, best of all, Rick asks to see the therapist because he no longer can bear what's going on, and his earlier meeting with the therapist gave him a sense that being helped is possible, that it exists.

Remember, rescue fantasies need to be analyzed, not enacted. Now that we're getting to look at some difficult treatment situations it becomes clear why child treatment demands an enormous need for flexibility, tact, and common sense.

QUESTION: Yes, and now you've defined one objective of the evaluation process as determining whether a family is ready for their child to be a patient, whether the parents will allow it, and whether the child will be receptive and able to make use of treatment. Did I get that right?

ANSWER: Yes. As we said earlier, *during the evaluation process we're evaluating the need for treatment, the identity of the patient, the readiness to begin at this time, and the best way to begin.*

QUESTION: What criteria do you use to determine whether a child needs treatment? My question now is directed solely at the emotional and developmental state of the child. I realize that the attitude of his parents will play a part in making a decision to proceed with treatment. But what about the child? When do we decide that a problem or a symptom warrants treatment, and when do we decide that it's perhaps just a phase that will pass with time?

ANSWER: Your question makes me realize how rarely we're consulted about a child who would not benefit from treatment providing that the attitude of the parents is conducive to such a plan.

QUESTION: Could you make a distinction between a child who would benefit from treatment and one who most clearly needs it?

ANSWER: I wish I could say that the degree of suffering experienced by a child should play a major part in making a distinction between benefiting from and needing treatment, but nothing in our work is that simple. Some children are so good at adapting that they adapt to the most awful situations, appear to be coping nicely, and do not appear to be suffering. Yet their adaptation is at a high price, the full measure of which might not become apparent until much later in their lives. Other children appear to suffer a great deal, but sometimes that suffering is transient. It could, for instance, be a reaction to a particular situation, such as the birth of a sibling, a serious illness, the death of a grandparent, and so forth. The transient suffering might well recede on its own or with the help of wise parents.

QUESTION: So if suffering is not in and of itself a good enough gauge, what is?

ANSWER: We have to look at the developmental picture as a whole. This is where you assess whether a child over the age of 7 has passed through the separation-individuation process and has more or less reached a state of object constancy (Mahler et al. 1975). And you assess whether she has navigated through the successive stages of psychosexual development, tackled the oedipal stage, and arrived at latency relatively intact, with adequate defenses and good ego functioning, or whether she has gotten seriously stuck at earlier crossroads and is limping along with skewed development.

If we go back to Rick and just look at his symptoms we can see right away that the overeating suggests many possibilities of development being derailed. Is the overeating suggestive of a fixation point at the oral stage, a primitive attempt at self-soothing, an expression of aggression in the form of devouring? The clumsiness is surely a sign of poorly defined body boundaries and suggests insufficient cathexis of the bodily self. The blushing is an oddly feminine, exhibitionistic, and pretty mysterious expression of some inner state not accessible to verbalization. Even viewed in this pretty speculative and superficial manner it's clear that Rick is lagging behind in his development to a profound degree and based on this alone he is a boy badly in need of treatment. His suffering is intense and might make him receptive to treatment.

In contrast, there are children like a girl I knew named Dawn, whose precocious ego development, accelerated as it was by the neglect of her alcoholic parents, gave her amazing poise and a high level of social awareness. These traits caused her to earn the respect of teachers and peers. Although Dawn's development, like that of Rick, was skewed, her vulnerabilities were well hidden. She presented herself to the world very differently than he did, and had attained a level of equilibrium that served her well. She would have been very reluctant to enter treatment and give up her hard-won coping mechanisms. Entering treatment would upset her carefully achieved counterphobic way of dealing with fear, her disavowal of longing, and her inability to regress in the service of the ego. Unlike Rick, she did not appear to need treatment; indeed she coped much better than he did. But her future development was very burdened by the level of control she maintained at all times, and that was subject to crack as the forces of the future were to unfold and perhaps tax her beyond her adaptive range. We rarely get to see children like Dawn. Their teachers respect and admire them, their parents exploit and ignore them, and they, in turn, take pride in their self-sufficiency. We might see Dawn at some point during adolescence, when her self-sufficiency is upset by her burgeoning sexuality. Any number of things might cause her to be referred to us. There is, for instance, the possibility that she becomes pregnant, seeks an abortion, and is referred to us by a wise doctor who recognizes something about her personality and present predicament.

My point is that many children whose development is skewed do not appear in our offices because they do not exhibit the symptoms that would call attention to them and to their need for help. Rick's need for treatment is very visible, and in that way he has a better chance of getting the help he needs, providing his parents allow that to happen.

QUESTION: Have you ever encountered a situation where you were consulted by a parent about a child and you felt that neither parent nor child needed help?

ANSWER: Yes. Whenever this has happened in my practice, the parent was in analysis, and often an analyst as well, and the child was very young. Analysts and analysands are more likely than the population at large to check out developmental hurdles in their children with a professional. Often these hurdles can be resolved in one or two consultations without ever seeing the child, or in some cases the child can be seen only once (Siskind 1997). These transient problems are the result of generally good enough parents running into a phase in the life of their child that was of special difficulty in their own childhood (Benedek 1959) and suddenly the unremembered is reenacted via the child.

QUESTION: Would you say that there is no single criterion in determining a child's need for treatment?

ANSWER: No, I'm saying something a bit different. I believe that a clear picture of his total development holds the criteria we need to make that determination. If we find a child's development becoming increasingly skewed, then he certainly is in need of treatment because it's unlikely that anything else will be able to reverse this unfortunate process. However we need to find a way to convince him and his parents that treatment is in his best interest and that's sometimes a tall order.

Some additional thoughts on your question about the difference between needing treatment and being able to benefit from treatment: certainly some situations appear more urgent than others and these differences are usually quite obvious. For instance, a child who is constantly in trouble and failing at whatever he attempts to do appears to be more in need of treatment than the quiet, good child who is chronically depressed. Is it not our job to help both of them to the best of our ability and theirs? I suspect that the notion of a child needing treatment versus being able to benefit from it is a false issue and not one we need be concerned about. If someone can benefit from treatment and live a better life because of it that's reason enough to seek it. It's bad enough that insurance agencies and the managed care industry attempt to make such decisions. We don't have to join them.

5

⤳

The Therapist's Findings and Recommendations

QUESTION: Having completed the evaluation process and having determined that a child would benefit from treatment, how do you decide on a treatment plan? How, for instance, do you decide that treatment should begin now, at this point in development, rather than in six months when new developmental gains might have been attained that ameliorate the situation? Or in other situations, waiting for a period of time after the occurrence of a traumatic event might allow some natural healing to take place and thus eliminate the need for treatment.

ANSWER: That's one of those big questions that sounds pretty overwhelming when raised without context. As soon as we begin to think about a specific child, his particular parents, and the situation or set of circumstances that brought him to our office, the question begins to feel much more manageable. When we think of the real people we've met and gotten to know, our thinking becomes anchored and gains structure and organization.

You ask what criteria we use to determine the timing of treatment. Well, there are some obvious situations wherein a child is suffering and his family is much affected by his distress and very anxious to have the help of a therapist. When child and parents are eager for help and the therapist feels qualified to offer that help, the decision to proceed with treatment is pretty straightforward. But that's the exception. Most situations are not so straightforward. But whatever the circumstances, even in those that seem clear cut, the reason for treatment should still be carefully examined by the therapist, conceptualized, and spelled out to both parents and child.

QUESTION: Can you give an example of a "simple" situation and then see how it could be conceptualized and explained to the parents?

ANSWER: Yes. I'm thinking of Seth, a boy of 7, who was very unhappy at school because he cried very easily and felt ashamed of this trait in himself. He wanted to be tough and big, not a "crybaby." He was a very likeable boy, playful, imaginative, intelligent, and curious. He was a good observer of people and insightful and perceptive in his observations. He seemed in all respects the kind of a child who would be popular with his peers and respected by both children and adults. But his tendency to cry so easily was not lost on some of his meaner classmates and they provoked his tears at every opportunity. This definitely reduced his standing with adults and children. His sensitive and caring parents tried to help him control his crying and general vulnerability to the rough-and-tumble ways of some of his classmates, but their efforts failed, and Seth continued to cry every day. Both parents worried about their son's self-esteem in light of the daily humiliation his crying was causing him and sought the help of a therapist.

So here we have what appears to be a "simple" situation: parents and child united in their quest to control the crying, and united in their expectation that this can be accomplished by psychotherapy for Seth and guidance for his parents.

QUESTION: Is this situation too ideal? Is there some other agenda that hasn't emerged yet?

ANSWER: Well, at this point we don't know. However, as mentioned before in earlier chapters, the presenting problem, the crying, is only the symptom. What is it a symptom of? Why does this very adequate, well-developing child have such a symptom? What role does it serve in his psychic economy? And what, if anything, do we tell Seth about our view of crying as a symptom? What do we tell his concerned and cooperative parents? We'd better be very clear about our own view of this before discussing it with Seth or his parents.

If we think of crying as a regression and take that idea a little further and speculate that Seth regresses in the face of hostile aggressive behavior on the part of his peers, we already have a working hypothesis. We can wonder whether we are witnessing the presence of a conflict around aggression that evokes overwhelming anxiety, thereby causing a regression to a younger, more helpless position. The formulation of this hypothesis is immediately helpful for it prompts us to explore something of this family's culture regarding aggression. Now suppose we discover that this is a very harmonious family; problems are solved by reason and compromise; there is very little fighting. This information can then lead to the speculation that aggression might not be well accepted in this family, that perhaps it's regarded as dangerous. With this thinking in place we might speculate that the crying is a symptom of separation anxiety, indicating that the use of aggression was curtailed during the separation-individuation process, leaving Seth fearful regarding his aggressive strivings. Consequently the use of this drive might seem so dangerous to Seth and evoke so much anxiety that it causes a regression to a younger and more dependent mode, which is expressed by the crying.

Of course the therapist must remember that she has arrived at this hypothesis based on a particular symptom within the context of a general picture of child and family, including the child's early history, some historical background about the parents, the current situation, observations of the child and parents, and a beginning understanding of the family dynamics. This hypothesis will either be borne out or proven inaccurate. It's important to have an open mind and not be invested in being right.

To get back to your earlier question about when to begin treatment, there is nothing in Seth's case to indicate that we should delay beginning and wait to see whether the problem will resolve on its own. Both parents and the child are eager to begin and there is no reason to delay.

Now we still have the second half of your question to address, and that was what to tell Seth and his parents about the purpose and goal of treatment. Since I've outlined an approach to thinking about this case, do you feel more equipped to formulate what we would say to Seth and his parents about treatment?

QUESTION: I still don't know what we would tell them, but I know we would first speak to the parents alone, and after sharing our recommendations with them, help them formulate what to tell Seth. Then at the next meeting with Seth we would tell him the reason for his treatment. As you can see I have some sense about the order of who to tell first, but I'm still very unsure about what and how much to tell.

ANSWER: I agree with the order you suggest, telling first the parents, then the child. I also like your question regarding how much to tell. After all, our insight into the situation is, at this point, speculative. We need a period of treatment to really illuminate the total situation: intrapsychic, inter-psychic, and environmental. It's best to begin by telling the parents what we've observed so far, and expressing it in a way that's helpful.

We cannot, must not, for a minute, forget that many parents feel anxious when coming to hear the findings and recommendations of a therapist. Most parents worry that they had done something harmful to their child and that this was now about to be exposed. The child might worry that he had done something "bad" and was about to be punished. Bearing this in mind, it is useful to make some general statements about the child and let the parents know you're aware of his strengths, of the big picture, rather than focusing exclusively on the problem area.

In the case of Seth, I would tell the parents that their son is a well-developing child with many strengths. He is intelligent, friendly, self-aware, imaginative, and full of ideas. Yet, as they know, something is getting in the way of his being comfortable in the world of his peers. In contrast, he is comfortable with adults, and he is comfortable in the area of learning. In fact, in all other areas of life he meets challenges well and deals with difficulties and frustrations with persistence and a healthy degree of confidence. It's only in the area of his peer relations that he gives up easily; that's when he cries. What we have to figure out in treatment is why this particular situation is so much more difficult for him than any other. As we begin to understand what's at play here, we can expect the beginning of a shift.

What Seth should be told is basically the same as what the parents are told but in a highly abbreviated version. It would be enough to tell him that there is a mystery in his life and it is this: he can be the boss of many things; for instance, he can be the boss of learning at school, and learning at home, like learning new games and using the computer. He is able to learn and understand a great deal about people and the world around him, does so all the time, every day. There is no question that he can figure out many, many things, but not the crying. Crying is something he hasn't been able to figure out or stop. Why this is so is a mystery. He hasn't been able to be the "boss" of crying and why that is so is something we're going to figure out together. That's going to be our job.

QUESTION: You make it sound very easy, yet even with a well-developing child and cooperative parents I imagine a therapist could present her findings in a way that could be very upsetting to child and parents and get the case off to a bad start. Could you say something about that, give some operating principle to avoid a bad beginning?

ANSWER: In a relatively benign situation, like the case of Seth, it's quite easy to formulate the reason for treatment. The operating principle here is to place the symptom—crying—within the larger context of Seth's life, highlighting his considerable sense of adequacy and strength in contrast to the one area where, despite their best efforts, the adults in his life are unable to help him. To present the need for treatment this way is really a matter of tact and common sense.

   No doubt all parents are pretty anxious about what we will have to say to them at the end of the evaluation process. They are apprehensive about what they might hear about their child, and indirectly about themselves. When we talk to them we must never forget that we are talking about their child. Being sensi-

tive to that fact goes a long way towards organizing what we're going to say and how we're going to say it—how our findings and recommendations are going to be presented to this particular couple.

You might have noticed that in my formulation I implied that once the problem is understood it should begin to shift. In the case of Seth I really believed that that would happen so I could say it with comfort. Some therapists are more cautious and perhaps not as optimistic, therefore they would never sound so confident of a good outcome. They would probably present a more measured version of their findings and not hold out as much hope as I did. In some cases it is indeed difficult to hold out much hope, at least until we've worked with child and parents for a period of time and know more about their situation and its potential for change. But the holding out of hope is also a matter of a therapist's personal style. I can't help but think that some of the very measured reports given to parents reflect a degree of stinginess and cautious self-protection on the part of some therapists, and not, as they might prefer to view it, a more careful adherence to the principles of *science*.

So, to answer your question, one could get off to a very bad start by not paying enough attention to the people involved, to their feelings and anxieties, and by not talking to them in a way that is both professional *and* friendly. Professional and friendly should not be a combination too hard to achieve. The two are quite compatible.

One could also get off to a bad start by failing to give careful thought to the information gathered, and failing to note blank spots, contradictory stories, affective behavior that's puzzling, and all manner of things that don't make sense. One would be in error in covering over some of these puzzles and inventing explanations, rather than recognizing that the therapist has been given a skewed picture, either to cover secrets or because of a particular pathological climate in which things don't fit together as they should.

I remember being startled by a father who had consulted me about his 5-year-old son. At some point in the session I asked this man about his own background. He told me a bit about his parents but didn't mention siblings, so I asked him if he had any. He told me that he had no sisters and then fell silent. I asked him whether he had any brothers and he nodded. "How many?" I asked. "Oh, four or five," he replied. I was so taken aback by "four or five" that I froze and failed to question this very odd response until several minutes later when I regained my equilibrium. I then learned that one brother had died during childhood. What eventually emerged was fear in the mind of this man that there was some deep similarity between his dead brother and his 5-year-old son.

And then there is always the issue of unrecognized countertransference as an obstacle to the therapist's clear thinking and behavior. A therapist could get off to a very bad start if he were unwilling to deal with his countertransferential responses to parents or child.

QUESTION: How would a therapist recognize his countertransference? If countertransference is unconscious, how do you recognize its presence?

ANSWER: We have to examine the reactions we have to all our patients and that of course includes the children we see in treatment and their parents. Some reactions are obvious to us while others are less directly experienced. For instance, we might find the brusque manner of a father off-putting, yet speculate that it's a defense he uses to ward off some state of anxiety that he cannot deal with any other way and we might become very interested in getting to know him in a deeper way. Or we might find the brusque manner of a father off-putting and find ourselves challenging him and behaving competitively with him. In this second reaction we have lost our professional equilibrium and are enacting a countertransferential drama.

In the example I just gave you about the father who said he had "four or five" brothers, my initial shock followed by avoidance was a countertransferential reaction. His statement tapped fear in me. Surprise, curiosity, and puzzlement would have been more ordinary reactions. My fear reaction was a clear signal to me that something very personal and inaccessible had been touched off.

Another example of countertransference is the most common one. The therapist becomes overidentified with the child, has rescue fantasies about being a better parent to that child, and conveys this to the child in various ways. I've mentioned this before and will no doubt mention it again. It cannot be stated too often. It is the greatest downfall of the child therapist, the greatest contribution to failed treatment of children.

QUESTION: Once you've established the need for treatment, the readiness of the parents to make this commitment, and the child's openness to the work ahead, how do you go about deciding things like frequency of appointments for both child and parents? How do you decide whether to see the parents together or separately?

ANSWER: Again, a question like this without the clinical context seems hard to answer, but when faced with a specific child and his parents it becomes a lot easier.

Let's begin with the issue of frequency of appointments for the child. Here we have to balance the requirements of the treatment situation with the realities of family life and what that means in terms of schedules and scheduling.

Let's first think a little about frequency of appointments. Freud saw his patients five or six times a week because he believed that the psychoanalytic method required this degree of intensity in order that the flow of free associations and dream interpretation not be subjected to interruptions that would "crust over" and impede the process of bringing into consciousness derivatives of unconscious fantasies. The intensity of the treatment was of paramount importance. This is still so regarding psychoanalysis, although frequency has generally dropped to four or even three sessions per week.

In the treatment of children, frequency used to parallel that of adult treatment. However, in recent years fewer and fewer children enter psychoanalytic treatment. In the past two decades parents appear to be unwilling to have their children attend such frequent sessions. For many of the more affluent parents, those who can afford the expense of psychoanalysis for their children, the idea of such intensive treatment appears to be in disfavor and even psychoanalytic psychotherapy at once or twice a week has to share the after-school schedule with piano and tennis lessons and the like, and not hold a place of higher importance as it did in the past. For poorer parents it is not an option offered by low-cost clinics or approved by managed care providers.

It appears that at present psychoanalytic psychotherapy has generally replaced psychoanalysis in the practices of child therapists trained psychoanalytically.[7] Unfortunately this shift in parental attitude is pretty common and not open to discussion, even in those cases where psychoanalytic treatment would be more effective.

QUESTION: Why is this happening? Aren't more frequent sessions preferable to ones farther apart?

ANSWER: As with anything else in our work, there is no simple answer. During this decade in the United States there is a

---

7. Other forms of psychotherapy such as behavior modification, group therapy, family therapy, attachment therapy, and others are practiced by professionals trained in those modalities, but since they fall outside the expertise of this author, they will not be discussed in this book.

reluctance among parents to have their children enter psychoanalysis. Parents seem very concerned with filling their children's after-school hours with all sorts of activities including every kind of imaginable lesson. Parents are placing much more emphasis on their children's *achievement*, starting at a young age. Parental anxiety appears to be high, as is a general tendency towards impatience. The slow pace of the psychotherapeutic process is very difficult for many parents.

When we make recommendations to parents we are doing so in the context of a culture that is resistant to this process. Consequently we should consider the child's treatment within the context of the total family situation, as well as from our understanding of the child's need for treatment and our assessment of his ability to make use of it. So we have to take a lot into account when we decide on a treatment plan.

QUESTION: This sounds very complicated. How do you know enough at the beginning to make such decisions?

ANSWER: You know enough to make tentative plans. For instance, you know that if the family has to travel over an hour each way to bring the child to his sessions and there are three other children in the family and no money for baby-sitters and no family members to help out, chances are that no matter how "good" frequent appointments might be, the family will not be able to manage more than once or twice per week sessions.

QUESTION: So you're saying that sometimes circumstances rather than the specific needs of the child will determine the frequency of appointments? That seems like a shame. What if once a week is not going to make a dent?

ANSWER: Well, there are circumstances where once a week would seem like very little, and yet, as in the case I just described, it's all the family can manage. Then you have to consider whether there is a therapist closer to their home who would eliminate some of the travel. That might be a solution. Sometimes a transfer like that could work very nicely. In some cases such a transfer might have been part of the plan all along, since the difficulties of travel would have been obvious and ongoing throughout the evaluation process.

QUESTION: Why would you undertake an evaluation with a family that's going to have so much difficulty getting to you because of distance? Wouldn't they be better off seeing someone close to home from the beginning?

ANSWER: Yes, you would think so, but all sorts of factors enter the picture. For instance, suppose these parents have heard very fine things about you and want only you to evaluate their child. In their enthusiasm they don't realize the burden that travel will impose. Another possibility is that the person who recommended you so highly to these parents had a child for whom treatment was not deemed necessary by you, and these parents were hoping that you would tell them that their child did not need treatment either.

The variations are endless. Of course, if a therapist knows from the beginning that travel arrangements are very burdensome, that's a subject that should be discussed during the first phone call, before you begin the evaluation. Some parents prefer to have one person do the evaluation and another do the treatment. They feel the evaluation will be more objective if the therapist has nothing personal to gain by recommending treatment.

The way we are viewed by many people is quite paradoxical. On the one hand we're expected to be utterly altruistic, available night and day, not needing vacations, unconcerned about money, and so forth. On the other hand our recommendations for treatment, suggestions for greater frequency of appointments, policies about charging for missed appointments, and occasional fee increases are all viewed as shamefully self serving. This is not a universal view of us, but it's one we run into quite often.

QUESTION: What about having one person do the evaluation and another the treatment? Is that a good plan?

ANSWER: Sometimes it's an excellent plan and sometimes it's not. I'll amplify my statement. I believe in most cases the evaluation process takes a great deal of skill and experience. I'm almost afraid to say this because there are so many exceptions, but here goes anyway. The evaluation is often a more difficult process than treatment proper. So in some cases a very experienced therapist might do the evaluation and if treatment is recommended, a more junior person might do a very good job of that, particularly if the therapist doing the treatment enters supervision or at least seeks consultation to enrich his work.

Now here's the other side of the picture regarding splitting the evaluation and the treatment. A lot happens during a thorough evaluation process. You meet with the parents and the child several times, the parents tell you a great deal about themselves and their child. The child meets a stranger who has been presented as having a helping role, and generally the meetings are rewarding for the child. A lot of attachments may form during this process, early transference reactions are activated, and if things have gone well, a working alliance is in the making. It could be very hard for the parents and child to leave a person who has become valued and go to someone else.

QUESTION: So what do you do if the parents can't manage optimal frequency of appointments? Do you see a child just once a week even if that seems insufficient? Or do you send the family to someone near their house whom they don't trust as much as they trust you?

ANSWER: These are some of the tough choices we have to make. It's a balancing act. How badly does the child need greater frequency? What do we know about the therapist who is well situated geographically? How realistic is the concern about travel? What are some of the transference–countertransference manifestations that might blur the therapist's decision-making perspective? Does the therapist *want* to treat this child and his parents?

QUESTION: The last point you made really surprised me. Do you really think about whether you want to treat a particular child?

ANSWER: What do you find surprising about that?

QUESTION: I never think about whether I want to treat someone. I might be aware of finding someone particularly interesting, attractive, or intimidating, but I don't take it any further. It feels somehow "not nice." I'm supposed to help people and not be selective about my patients. How can I accept some and reject others?

ANSWER: It's not a bad question to ask yourself: "Do I want to treat this person?" It opens up some awareness of countertransferential material and that's always valuable. But beyond the countertransference is also a very real situation. Treatment is usually a long-term commitment. We do have to give some thought to the patients we take on, often for many, many years. And we have to think about the combination of patients we see in a given day. A child therapist who sees seven or eight children in one day would be pretty worn out and not very effective if all these children had poor impulse control and had to be restrained from trashing her office. She might manage establishing a therapeutic climate with one or two or three such children, but if dealing with out-of-control behavior was the whole day's work, her role might gradually change to just containing these demanding children, keeping them busy with time-passing games, rather than helping them use language and thought in place of action and physical discharge.

I know therapists don't always have a choice, especially in clinic settings. And now, in private practice, the encroachment of managed care has restricted the pool of patients who seek treatment outside of clinics. Consequently, the pool has grown smaller and with it the shrinkage in everyone's ability to make choices. But despite the reality of reduced choices, it's still good to ask ourselves whether we want to take on a particular case and then explore our answer. We might not always act on it but it's sure to inform us in a helpful way.

QUESTION: What would make you reluctant to take on a child case after having completed the evaluation?

ANSWER: In most cases my reluctance would have more to do with the parents than the child. If I felt that both parents had a hostile attitude toward me I would have trouble accepting the case. I would discuss this with them and do my best to understand the underlying dynamics, but if this did not budge I would tell them quite frankly the reason we should not work together.

QUESTION: What would you tell them?

ANSWER: I would tell them that the outcome of their child's therapy depends a great deal on their attitude about treatment and on our ability to work together regarding their child. I would tell them that I don't think that they feel comfortable with me. That would make it hard for them to trust that their child is in good hands. I would tell them it must be very distressing to feel that they must send their child to someone they don't have confidence in. If they feel compelled to accept such a plan, that sounds pretty intolerable. I would then suggest they meet some other therapists and find one they feel more comfortable with. I would offer to help them find someone else.

QUESTION: What if they told you they don't trust therapists in general and another therapist would not make any difference so you might as well do it?

ANSWER: I might suggest spending some time exploring their distrust prior to making a final decision or I might tell them that I would not be able to work under such circumstances. This is a situation where I would carefully take my own feelings about the matter into consideration.

QUESTION: Could you mention some other situations where at the end of the evaluation you would not take on the case?

ANSWER: Sometimes parents make unacceptable conditions for treatment. One father told me that he "owns" the content of his 5-year-old daughter's sessions since he pays for them. Therefore he wants a full report of what transpires between us. Another parent, a very ambitious and status-oriented mother, wanted the names of the schools and colleges my children, my husband, and I attended. She said she was afraid I might not have as high standards as she did and this information would either reassure her or disqualify me. I was once asked by a father to falsify my bill so the insurance company would pay more and he would pay less.

QUESTION: Were you able to work anything out with the three examples you just mentioned?

ANSWER: Actually, although I refused to do as asked in all three instances, all of the parents accepted my refusal to comply with their demands, and all three cases got under way. The father who wanted to know exactly what his daughter had to say only attended two of his weekly sessions over a three-year-period. On those two occasions he came more than thirty minutes late. The second time he came he told me his sole reason for coming to see me was to tell me that he held me responsible for his daughter's recent weight gain. He did not like fat children and did not think being fat was good for anyone. He would not continue sending her to me. He proceeded to send her to various other therapists, always pulling her out after a few months and always leaving an unpaid bill.

The mother who wanted information about the schooling of each member of my family was able to address her anxiety and that case went well but partly for the wrong reason. Her daughter was accepted into the mother's first-choice school and I was given credit for this success. Although this was not credit I deserved, it did reduce the mother's resentment toward treatment enough to allow her daughter to continue working with me until she no longer needed me. Our termination was planned and we ended with a lot of good work accomplished.

The father who wanted me to falsify my bills said he could understand that I might not be willing to be "flexible" in this way. He had heard that "shrinks" tended to be "rigid." He brought his son for treatment and then failed to pay his bill. After two months I told him I could not work and not get paid. He said he could understand that very well, he wouldn't like it either. He proceeded to terminate his son's treatment.

QUESTION: If you had to do it over again, would you change anything you did?

ANSWER: Yes, I would ask myself whether I wanted to work with any of these parents. Had I done that I would have said "no" to the two fathers and "maybe" to the mother. But I don't mean to imply that the therapist's personal preference is always a good indicator of outcome. It's only one of many factors. However in the treatment of adults we have much more opportunity to work on difficulties that arise. Discord between patient and analyst become part of the analytic playing field, the subject of extensive analysis. In work with the parents of our child patients we're limited in our ability to do this sort of exploration. Not infrequently this leaves us with discord that festers, impedes the progress of the case, and often results in premature termination.

QUESTION: Let's go back to the issue of frequency. If the parents are well disposed towards treatment and there are no travel time and expense obstacles, how often would you want to see a child and how often would you want to see his parents? Would you see the parents together or separately?

ANSWER: I don't like to see children less than twice per week. In some cases three times a week is better. If a child is very anxious and/or very depressed we would place that as uppermost in importance and arrange for very frequent appointments, three or four times a week or even more if the situation is very extreme.

Sometimes it just isn't possible to see the child more than once per week and if that's the case we accept it and see what happens. If it seems that once a week is just not productive, then that second appointment time has to be found even if it requires a very early before-school appointment or some other less than ideal time. Sometimes we have to see a child during school hours, but that should not be done lightly. It should be a last resort.

The frequency of a child's appointment need not be fixed forever. In many cases we might begin with once a week and move to twice, or begin with twice and move to once. The child's ability to use treatment would be a determining factor as well as the nature of the problem and its impact on the child's life. For instance, Seth was basically a healthy child with a particular problem that was manifested in his readiness to cry. But this symptom caused him and his parents so much distress that it occupied a large portion of their daily life. Treatment was invested with the hope of change and was highly valued. Seth had two sessions a week but his sessions had much reach into the time between. He really thought about what we discussed and did a remarkable amount of work on his own. Had he not had that ability I would probably have wanted to see him for a third weekly session.

QUESTION: How often did you see his parents? Did you see them together or separately?

ANSWER: I would like you to first consider why I needed to see his parents and then the how often will follow. Much as these parents valued treatment, it was still quite a wrench for them to need to rely on a therapist. A stranger was now going to do what they could not. They needed to stay in the picture, not be excluded, and make a contribution. They needed to feel that we were working together toward a common goal. They gave me important information about life at home and provided their observations of Seth. This was helpful, but perhaps more in terms of solidifying our working alliance than from any great need for this gathering of information. At the beginning I saw the parents, each separately, every other week and together about every six weeks. After a while the individual parent sessions were reduced to once a month and the joint session remained the same. This worked out well.

In some situations we would see the parents more often. We would not always see each parent at the same frequency. Sometimes we would only see the parents together because they might very much prefer to have joint appointments. We would have to be clear about why we needed to see them and then propose a plan and negotiate that plan so that it suited them. There is no formula to determine the ideal frequency of appointments for child or parents. It's more a matter of being clear about our objectives and placing a high emphasis on the maintenance and enrichment of the working alliance.

The

Treatment

Process

6

᷒

The Child Therapist's Office: Selection and Use of Play Materials

QUESTION: What kind of toys and equipment should a child therapist have? Are some materials particularly effective in encouraging self-expression? What toys are useful in promoting communication with the children we see in consultation and in treatment?

ANSWER: Yes, there are definitely toys that lend themselves well to diagnostic observation and play therapy whereas others do not. Since we want to select what is most useful to our work, we need to look at toys from the perspective of their potential role in the therapeutic situation. That means choosing play materials that are open ended and restricting those that impose a particular theme or have prescribed rules. For instance, wooden blocks can be used to build anything the child wishes, whereas a doll house suggests the theme of aspects of family life. An example of a particularly restrictive material is the typical board game with its prescribed purpose and set of rules.

In general, board games are not the most useful materials since they do not lend themselves to enhancing communication, which, after all, is our primary purpose. However, there are circumstances in which a board game comes in handy because the child we're working with does not want to communicate with us. A board game would give him the means to protect himself from our interest in him.

QUESTION: Are you saying that under certain circumstances you would provide a child with play material that might aid his resistance to treatment?

ANSWER: Yes, in a way I am saying that, although I would not want to use the term *resistance* in this context. Resistance is one of those words that has a general meaning to the public at large and a specific meaning in psychoanalytically oriented discussions. Remember, it's a term used by Freud to describe the analysand's *unconscious* opposition to the various forms of self-knowledge that are the normal part of the psychoanalysis or psychotherapy of adults. In our discussion I would rather reserve that term for its very specific use.

To conclude our discussion of board games I would simply say that some children might feel very anxious at being alone with the therapist and would need to have a way of *avoiding* the intensity of the situation, at least at the beginning of treatment. A board game might give them the emotional protection they seek.

But let's look a little deeper and examine what I just said in the context of a clinical situation concerning a real child who is extremely anxious. You'll see that by having a board game on hand what we've really done turns out to be the opposite of supporting the patient's avoidance, or eventually, resistance to treatment. We've allowed a frightened child to enter treatment at his own pace and in the only way he could without suffering intense anxiety.

Let's say our patient is a boy named Josh and he's 8, shy, and terrified of strangers and strange situations. Let's say he hates being brought to his therapist's office, and will not talk or play with the "good toys" offered. Furthermore he gives his parents a very hard time every time they have to bring him to his session. In fact, they're at their wit's end about how to get him out of the house and into the car for the trip to his therapist, and then out of the car once they've arrived at the therapist's office. And that's not where the difficulty ends, for once in the waiting room it's hard to move him into the office, and when that's done he sits there sullen, miserable, and monosyllabic.

Suppose we know from his parents that he loves the game "Chutes and Ladders." Might we not decide that while the game is not useful in the usual sense of promoting self-expression and communication, it might help Josh feel more comfortable in this situation? I think you'll agree that this would be reason enough to make use of a board game, despite its limitations.

This example illustrates how open minded we have to be at all times. You asked me a straightforward question about play materials and no sooner had I mentioned a general rule that's usually useful, than in the next moment we ran into an exception to it.

QUESTION: Let's go back to my original question then. What are some good toys to have in a child therapy office?

ANSWER: I will give you a list of useful materials, but before I do, let me conceptualize the purpose of having these toys on hand. Then my list will have more meaning.

We talked about some of the difference between child and adult treatment. Children often don't know why they're being brought to a therapist, and even when we explain the reasons, it's often still unclear to them. And even if they do

understand why they've come, they are generally not articulate in expressing their feelings or in describing family dynamics. We can't expect them to sit in a chair and tell us
their concerns. What we can do is give them a setting that
allows them to become involved in play. Through their play
we get to know them better and are able to be helpful to
them. I realize how elementary this must sound to you; after
all it's something so basic to every child therapist. Still, surprising as it may sound, we all sometimes tend to forget the
purpose of the selection and use of the play materials we
have on hand.

The objective of providing these useful toys is obviously
not for our young patients' entertainment. Yet, feeling en-
tertained is a form of being engaged and we do want our
young patients to feel engaged in their play. The state of
being engaged indicates that the child is feeling relatively
safe, and if having fun is part of that state, that's not a bad
thing at all. The point is to find a balance between being
absorbed in playing for the sake of fun and being absorbed
in play and also furthering the therapeutic work.

I'm sometimes taken aback when a mother or father tells
me: "Karen just loves her appointments with you. She has
such a good time when she comes to see you. She asks every day whether it's one of her appointment days." What
surprises me is how pleased and sincere the parent sounds
about this, how accepting of the notion that a good time is
what goes on during the session. I sometimes have to squelch
my impulse to say that a good time is not what therapy is
about. It's a good thing I stop myself from presenting the
parent with my more *accurate* and *serious* view of treatment.
After all, that would be a countertransference enactment on
my part. The parent has made me into an *entertainer*, which
perhaps I feel to be a demotion, so I then respond with an
educational statement that reminds the parent that the child
is in need of *serious* help. In other words, I respond to being
put down with a retaliatory put down. That's a sure indica-

tor that I'm in trouble and that I'm going to cause trouble if I don't take a good look at what I'm doing with that parent.

There are a lot of reasons that might cause a parent to need to view me as a provider of a good time. Perhaps that's the only way that parent can tolerate my role in the life of her family. Perhaps seeing me as being there in response to a serious problem is too painful. If that's the case, it's usually best to leave that alone.

QUESTION: But don't some parents resent the idea that their children are having all that fun during their sessions, rather than doing "serious work"?

ANSWER: Absolutely. Some parents have just the opposite attitude and don't want their children to like the process, don't understand the role of play in their child's treatment, and feel it to be a waste of time.

QUESTION: I can see how complicated it gets. I never realized that the parents also react to the toys and equipment with positive and negative feelings. What do you do about that?

ANSWER: You pay careful attention to it, as you do to everything else that happens in treatment.

But now let me present you with a basic list of useful toys. Later we can talk some more about parental reaction to toys and how we might work with that.

Toys chosen for play therapy should be simple and should not be presented in great quantity. We know that most children are imaginative and can turn anything at hand into whatever it is they need for play. Our office need not look like a nursery school or an after-school gym program. A few shelves holding a discreet selection of toys are enough. Ideally these shelves are covered by curtains or behind doors so that the toys are not too prominently displayed.

I like to have groupings of toys in baskets or boxes on my shelves. Most of the toys are geared to younger children up to age 8 or 9. I'll say more about toys for children over 10 in a little while.

I don't like anything too commercial, such as Barbie dolls or wind-up toys or things that are generally advertised a lot on television. I tend to choose more basic toys, more old-fashioned toys, the kind you buy in stores that supply nursery schools. Here's what I've had on hand for years and find to work very well.

1. A basket containing finger puppets of familiar people in our lives, such as policemen, firemen, doctors, farmers, nurses, teachers, and storekeepers.
2. A basket of family people: a mother figure, a father figure, several child figures of different ages, several other adults of undetermined profession, and older grandparent figures. These are made of rubber and can be made to stand up or sit down.
3. A basket of rubber and plastic babies with little beds and carriages, blankets, and baby bottles.
4. A basket of wild animals.
5. A basket of farm animals.
6. A small collection of Playmobil™ toys and Lego™ toys.
7. Some hand puppets of people and animals.
8. A basket of manipulative toys that can be used for building interesting shapes.
9. A basket with cowboys and Indians.
10. A collection of small cars and trucks and a motorcycle.
11. A box of dominos, two decks of cards, and a set of pick-up sticks.
12. A sturdy wooden box filled with small wooden blocks. The scale of these blocks matches the size of all the cars, trucks, people, and animals. This makes it possible to build roads and bridges for the cars and trucks, homes with beds and

furniture for the people, farms and zoos for animals, and so forth.

13. Plenty of colored and white paper, pencils, pens, magic markers, excellent safe scissors, a fine heavy stapler, and a heavy tape dispenser that works well even in the hands of young children.

14. A box full of scraps of fabric and some needles and thread. These scraps have been useful for making blankets, curtains, clothing, hammocks, and so forth.

I want to stress that all these toys, while not elaborate or expensive, are of good quality and are kept in good repair. They are always neatly sorted into their baskets and placed in their special same position on my shelves.

QUESTION: What about books, puzzles, and action equipment such as a basketball hoop and ball to go with it?

ANSWER: Hidden away in a locked closet which is not in view I do have some books, a puzzle, and a couple of board games that I needed at some point in the past for a particular child. I keep them should the need for them arise again. As far as a basketball hoop and ball are concerned, I understand they're used by therapists with certain hyperactive children who are deemed incapable of doing without them, even for forty-five minutes. In some cases that's probably true, but I suspect these action toys are offered reflexively to certain kids and I would like to see this tradition reconsidered.

QUESTION: What objection do you have to action toys? You sound as if they rarely have a purpose, and yet basketball, bowling balls, miniature hockey games and such are commonly used with young adolescent boys. What's wrong with them?

ANSWER: Since you already know they're widely used it's obvious that some therapists consider them useful and that my perspective would not find consensus.

   I think these action games might be useful under some circumstances, particularly at the beginning of treatment with an adolescent who is not the least bit motivated to sit down and talk about things. Some adolescents have never in their lives sat down to talk things over. It's not part of their internal or external culture. The awkwardness of the treatment situation without an avenue of escape into physical action might be very daunting to some of these kids, and in such circumstances I can see a point to this approach. It allows the young person to rely on something familiar within the strangeness of the therapy situation. *I object to the repetitive and exclusive use of action games because they do nothing to promote a shift from action to thinking, from drive discharge to formed thoughts. A young person, male or female, who has reached early or mid-adolescence and cannot express himself verbally, or be reflective, or identify how he feels, and who hasn't developed the ability to think clearly and sequentially, is in trouble. This person is really not equipped to deal with the world as it is. Therapy offers the opportunity to do some developmental catching up. It shouldn't be squandered.*

QUESTION: But what about the relationship that develops between the therapist and the youngster while they shoot baskets? Perhaps this is the first adult the youngster has ever trusted and felt comfortable with. If the therapist curtailed their activity, wouldn't that compromise the bond that had formed?

ANSWER: That's a little like asking if the bond between mother and child wouldn't be compromised when the mother introduced weaning or toilet training, or required that her child dress himself. *Parents and therapists have some features in common. When parents have certain expectations of their chil-*

dren and therapists of their patients, child and adult, and when these expectations are reasonable and well timed, they're growth-promoting. The growth they encourage is achieved by the ego-fueled action of mastery required to reach the expectations and is further enhanced by the recognition of the respect that prompted the expectation. The youngster whose therapist finds a way to curtail the time spent playing ball has been offered something valuable in its place. Sure there might also be a sense of loss, but growth is like that.

QUESTION: Would there be something analogous to that in the use of materials with a very young child? Would we have a similar goal of moving from play to thought?

ANSWER: Not necessarily. Some children, although very young, are already thoughtful and articulate. Some of them are hypervigilant and hyperobservant. In fact, with some of these precocious children who are inhibited in the nonverbal sphere we might have the reverse goal, that of helping them feel free enough to play and to have a sense of abandon.

On the other hand there is the child I described earlier, 8-year-old Josh, who only wanted to play "Chutes and Ladders" and I thought it best to let him, since it was the only way to get him to come to sessions without major war and strife. "Chutes and Ladders" is a little like the basketball game; it has a use but eventually what was once useful may become an obstacle to further movement. The therapist has to gauge when to curtail the use of the board game; the negotiations that flow out of that exchange become the stuff of treatment.

QUESTION: How do you know when to begin curtailing something?

ANSWER: What a big question! Sometimes we don't know. And then sometimes we get little clues, if we're alert to them. Take, for instance, this example. For three months Josh has entered the room and headed straight for the "Chutes and Ladders" box on the shelf. Then one day Josh grabs it with his right hand as usual, but his left hand picks up a little truck, which he rolls back and forth a couple of inches forward and a couple of inches backward. In that moment you know he's not hanging on to "Chutes and Ladders" in the same way. You know there's been a shift. The same sort of thing can happen with your basketball player. One day he bounces into your office and flops down in your chair and tells you that he's beat, and you ask him what happened to tire him out. He tells you, without heading for the hoop and positioning himself to catch the ball, that there was a fight outside his bedroom and he couldn't sleep. Wait to see what he does next. Don't reflexively throw him the ball. This is a big moment, let it be . . . wait and let him make the next move.

QUESTION: Suppose Josh resumes "Chutes and Ladders," or suppose my basketball player is finished talking after his uncharacteristic statement and ready to shoot baskets. Then what? Do you try to curtail either of these patients in returning to their customary activities?

ANSWER: Not necessarily. What we're talking about here is not so different from the judgment and clinical decisions we make with our adult patients. With adults we're constantly choosing when to move in with an intervention and when to allow the patient's material to flow undisturbed. We have to do the same with our child and adolescent patients.

We know that when Josh picked up that little car, no matter that it was for thirty seconds, he was for those seconds a little less anxious than before, and the reduction in his anxiety level allowed him to make a spontaneous gesture. It's likely that saying nothing might be the best course of action with a child like Josh. Making a comment about his curiosity about the car might make him feel self-conscious and cause him to retreat. It might be best to do nothing and let the situation evolve. Or, one might say something offhand like "that's the oldest of my cars, the yellow one is the newest."

The reason I consider making an intervention like that is that it acknowledges that Josh did something different, but it places the attention on the inanimate object, the car, and not on Josh. Think of how different that might feel to a very frightened child than saying: "I see you're interested in my car." Or even more intrusive: "That's the first time you've ever shown interest in any toy other than 'Chutes and Ladders'."

Remember that with Josh, who cannot stand too much closeness, we have to keep our distance. Our failure in that regard could be our most serious blunder. The situation with our basketball player might be different; with him it might be fine to just say something like: "That sounds like some fight, Do you know what it was?" If he doesn't want to talk about it he can just shrug and resume shooting baskets.

If we're alert to the clues we're given, our clinical decisions have some basis. Of course, however alert we are we still make mistakes. Some mistakes are slighter than others and don't do much harm. What we don't want to do is push across a barrier that wasn't ready to come down. That kind of mistake could send us back to square one, or worse.

As you can see, so much of what may appear as *practical* in our work, like the selection of play materials, is rarely just that. When we look more deeply we realize that it's conceptual, that we're making choices that are an organic part of the whole. By the whole I mean the climate and process of treatment.

I hope I've given you a fairly clear idea of the selection of toys I've found adequate to our work. My general feeling is that we can do very well with a small selection of toys.

QUESTION: You said earlier that you prefer to have curtains or doors on your play therapy equipment shelves. Why?

ANSWER: I see children in an office that I also use for adult patients. I think it might be distracting to my adult patient to be in an office with shelves of toys in full view. But that's only one reason for having the toys covered. Even more important is the effect of these shelves of toys in full view to my child patients. It could seem like an enticement, an invitation to play rather than to talk.

We are creatures of habit in our work as well as in other areas of life. I was trained a certain way[8] and have stuck with it because it made good sense to me. The thinking for having doors or curtains on shelves was as follows:

The first time the child comes to the therapist's office the curtains or doors are open and the toys are in full view. Then, at all subsequent times that the child comes, the doors are closed and the toys are not in view; the child has to take the initiative of making them available. Most children really like the act of opening the doors (or curtains) and finding everything there, week after week, each toy in the same place as before. They seem to enjoy a proprietary feeling and a sense of predictability from this simple action. And of course, they may choose not to go to the toys right away, or at all.

QUESTION: What do you do when one of your child patients wants to take home a therapy toy?

ANSWER: I say "no." I don't let them. The first time they ask me I tell them that one of the therapy rules is that all the toys stay in the office. When they ask me again I remind them of this important therapy rule. When they ask me over and over again I refer to this rule in various ways: "Did you forget our rule?" "I can't believe you forgot. You have too

---

8. At the Child Development Center of the Jewish Board of Family and Children's Services.

good a memory to forget a rule like that." "Were you checking out whether I forgot? I would never forget such an important rule," and so forth. When they ask me the reason for this rule I tell them one of the special features of therapy is that everything is always the same when they arrive. The room looks the same, the toys are the same, and I'm the same in all my special ways, like not answering the telephone, and not doing anything other than paying attention to our time together. I tell them that the sameness of therapy is very important. Every time they come to see me they know what to expect from me and from the way I keep the room for them.

I'm sure you get the idea, but let me respond to your question in a conceptual way. *The therapist and the therapeutic situation offer the child a very reliable and predictable environment. One of our most important attributes is our offering a safe climate, one in which it becomes possible to express some not-so-safe feelings and thoughts.*

I have found that my refusal to let children take things home has been very useful in maintaining this predictable milieu. I present myself as the guardian of "an average expectable environment" (Hartmann 1939) *and I do it with absolute conviction.* I withstand the most heart-rending appeals:

> "But I need it, I can't go to sleep without this truck. If I had this truck I would never have nightmares because I'd know I had a getaway truck for when the bad guys come."

Or simply:

> "I need it very very badly, and if you don't give it to me I'll die and it will be your fault!"

My answer to that last appeal was:

> "Wouldn't it be terrible if I really believed that you would *die* if you didn't have this truck!? I wouldn't be much help to you if I believed a thing like that! Why the next thing might be that you'd believe it too!"

QUESTION: What about the things the children make during therapy? Do you let them take home pictures they draw or things they construct out of paper? What about stories they might write while they're with you, or if they're too young to write, stories they dictate to you? Can they take those home?

ANSWER: No. I tell them the things they make stay in the office. They're part of our therapy work and we need them to stay with us. I provide my patients with boxes and/or folders for their art work and stories and these items are kept in my office for them in absolute privacy.

QUESTION: Are you as strict about their art work going home with them as you are about their never being allowed to borrow your office toys?

ANSWER: Almost, but not quite. For instance, sometimes a child will want to make a card for a parent's birthday or other special occasion. Sometimes I'll agree to that and sometimes I won't. It depends on the circumstances, but I never agree to such a thing on the spot. If something were to go home we would have discussed it over a period of time to make sure it really warranted making an exception. I would be guided by two principles here. The first is my awareness of how important this exception to the rule might be to the child. Would it be unsettling for her to have me break my own rule? Would any circumstance warrant that? Would it make me less reliable, less strong, less safe? These would be some of the questions I might ask myself and perhaps also ask the child. It would take us into a whole process of examining something together in a very deep way, a really important process in itself, whatever the decision.

My other concern, and it's not unrelated, would be to check out whether this request might be just a ruse to get me to break my own rule. Obviously it isn't good for my young patients to feel they can outsmart me, at least not outsmart me too often. So you see, I'm careful about such requests, and in most cases there is no need to break the rules. Children have so many other opportunities to make a card for their mom or dad or whoever was the subject of their request.

Also, as we enter the termination process, my young patients and I usually go through all the things they've made that I've saved for them. It's an interesting and useful experience to remember together when certain things were made, and why and how things have changed since then. During this review the child chooses what to throw out and what to keep, and what is kept may be taken home on their last appointment.

QUESTION: What is the basis of your rule that children in treatment not take home their therapy products?

ANSWER: It's not so different from the reason we like our analysands not to discuss their dreams outside of treatment. It takes away from the intensity of the therapeutic relationship and therapeutic work. It dilutes and trivializes important communications. Sometimes a picture might be just a squiggle or a few dots but a whole story might have been told while the picture was being made. Sometimes a child will place a single dot or a line on twenty sheets of paper just to see what I will do about it. It's a way of testing this new adult, this stranger. This kind of exchange can have important meaning, but it would only be meaningful to the child and his therapist.

That brings us to the next reason bringing art work home from therapy sessions is not a good idea; it involves parents in a nonhelpful way. Parents might resent having piles of art work from therapy now joining piles of art work from school. They might wonder why they're paying so much money and going to so much trouble to provide their child with an opportunity to scribble. Stories brought home from therapy might portray them unsympathetically or have frightening themes. There are so many reasons to keep therapy productions where they belong—in the therapy office.

QUESTION: What about children bringing their own toys to the therapist's office? Do you have any objection to that?

ANSWER: No, I would accept it and view it as a communication. But I would want to know why the child had chosen to bring that toy to show me. My wanting to know doesn't mean that I get told. I might not be told a thing about it, but then I would perhaps say to the child: "You brought this truck to show me. That must mean it's special in some way, but you aren't saying what you would like me to see when I look at it. Now I'm wondering what it is that you aren't saying. So now we have a mystery. That truck is about something. Is it that you don't know how to say it, or that you want to have a secret? This really is a mystery, and maybe we'll get to solve it someday."

That way, the child's action in bringing a truck or any other item from home is clearly viewed as a communication and that in turn is conveyed to the child. It's another of the many things that make a therapist different from other people. Other people are much freer with their comments, much more likely to say: "Oh look at that nice truck." We know the truck isn't necessarily nice, it might be part of a destructive fantasy or a rescue fantasy, or limitless other possibilities. We just can't know until we're told or see the fantasy played out.

QUESTION: And if the child asks to leave the truck in your office until next time, or for a long time, do you let him?

ANSWER: Maybe. It would be discussed and if the child needed it in his play and if it could be put in his special box, out of sight between sessions, I would agree to it. I would not agree to very large items that I could not put out of sight since I would not want other children to see something that belonged to another child and was off limits to them.

QUESTION: What if it was small enough to join your cars and trucks in your basket of such toys?

ANSWER: No, I would not allow children to add to my selection of toys. I'm the only one who chooses play therapy toys. That would be a rule.

QUESTION: I think I know the answer to this question, but to make sure let me ask it. What do you say when a child wants you to tape up one of his pictures?

ANSWER: "No." Is that what you expected me to say?

QUESTION: Yes. During the course of this discussion you've talked about the importance of keeping the room the same, and not sharing with others what's produced during the course of your work together. That would definitely be on the side of not having children's art work on your walls.

I have one more question about toys. What toys do you have for children over 10?

ANSWER: Very few. I have cards, dominos, drawing and writing materials, and pick-up sticks. If necessary I can provide a checker set and a chess set, but I'm reluctant to do that since chess, especially, takes a long time to play and requires a great deal of attention. Some card games are so easy that they become a background to conversation. I find that most useful. With children over 10 it's very useful to talk and not have too many things around that will interfere with verbal communication.

I find that some older children are able to sit in the adult chair and just talk and converse the entire session. Other 10 and older children prefer sitting at my desk and using a card game or checkers as the background to our conversation.

QUESTION: Is it your goal to help the children who play while they talk give up the play and just talk?

ANSWER: No, not at all. You know, that's another one of those questions like do I prefer to get the parent out of the room as soon as possible so as to be alone with the child. The real point is that I want to get to know the child as well as possible at the pace he sets for this process. His pace is as much a part of the story as his secrets, fantasies, and deepest wishes. I just want to get to know him and what it's been like for him. Then we can look at things together; then we are occasional allies joined in a mission, and occasional enemies, because what we do can be very hard and sometimes he wants no part of it. But that's the way the process goes sometimes, and when it goes that way we can begin to use a serious word like *resistance*. Much as the child wants to change and feel more adequate and independent, these are areas of great conflict, and in the course of treatment the multiple sides of conflict appear and disappear.

QUESTION: You're making it sound more like the treatment of adults. Is that what happens? Does it become more like adult treatment once the child is engaged in the process?

ANSWER: There are essential similarities between the treatment of children and that of adults. Treatment at all ages is sometimes very hard, sometimes illuminating, sometimes frightening, sometimes very exciting, and so forth. *What we are interested in is how to use toys and play to promote a treatment situation rather than having the playing become an after-school activity aimed at spending time in a pleasant way. What we are trying to achieve and understand is the transformation of play into therapeutic work.*

CHAPTER

7

⤳

A Child's First Session

QUESTION: Could you talk about a child's first session? Should we have any particular goals in mind in thinking about this event?

ANSWER: You called a first session an "event" and I think you had good reason for choosing that word, for it is an important "event" . . . important for the child and for the therapist as well. After all, it's the end point of one process, the evaluation, and the beginning of another, treatment proper.

Let's think for a minute about all that preceded that first session. In a typical case, when that first session takes place it marks the completion of a time frame during which the child's behavior or affect caused him to be identified by his parents, or by his teacher, or possibly by other significant adults in his life, as being in need of help, and this has then been confirmed by you, the therapist. That suggests that the child has been struggling or unhappy or sad or frightened or feeling inadequate or in much conflict or depressed for some time, and now, after a careful period of evaluation during which he has met you once or twice or three times, here he is in your office on this Tuesday afternoon at four o'clock and will be in your office again on Friday at four o'clock. This is the place and the time where the two of you will meet week after week to talk, to play, and to figure out why things got so difficult and how to make them better. On Tuesdays and Fridays, the four o'clock hour will belong to this child, to be with you for as long as he needs to come. Ideally, that is.

QUESTION: As you talk about a first session and particularize it just a bit, I can hear in your description a certain tone. What you say is very simple and very obvious, and yet the total effect conveys a viewpoint that feels very helpful to me. It's helpful to think of all the turmoil and work on the part of the family to make that first session possible. And then it's finally here, and the therapist and the child are together in that room, the therapist providing a setting for what is to unfold, the child looking around, getting his bearings, and eventually moving into play. The therapist is at first in the background, attuned to what's developing, staying in step with the child as the two of them begin to make their way into the not-yet-known. Is that what you had in mind?

ANSWER: This time you got way ahead of me. I was just saying what I knew so far, the obvious as you plainly put it. But you're right, I am expressing an attitude of something unhurried, leisurely, something that doesn't strain. Yes, I see the therapist as providing the setting. The child will provide the action, the tone, the themes, and the content. He will do it in his time and at his pace.

For some children, being able to set the pace and tone is in itself a major departure from how they have lived their lives: not to have to rush to keep up, not to have to fit into a preset agenda, and not to have to be found wonderful . . . or disappointing, for either one is pretty awful. The therapy situation affords the child a chance to just be, and that's a new experience for many children. For some, a quiet room and a responsive and respectful adult immediately feels very different, welcoming and perhaps even hopeful. But while this is so for some children, for others this quiet partnership might feel quite the opposite; it might feel claustrophobic, engulfing, and terrifying.

QUESTION: So do you present treatment differently to children whose response to the treatment setting would be at such extremes from each other?

ANSWER: Yes and no. The spirit of treatment is the same and we would try to capture that in the way we introduced the child to beginning therapy, but what we would actually say would vary in order to fit what we already know and continue to learn about the particular child. Remember that when the child comes for his first session you aren't completely in the dark; he's already known to you from the evaluation process. This child has been to your office before. He has revealed something of himself to you. So you will already have a pretty good idea of how to regulate the closeness–distance space between you.

QUESTION: What do you mean by the closeness–distance space between us?

ANSWER: Some children feel comfortable in the presence of another person, or at least relatively comfortable. Being with someone is not their problem area. They can talk and play fairly easily. This is apparent right away from their bearing and manner, from the way they look at you when they talk to you and look at you when you talk to them. But some children are strikingly anxious and shy. They don't talk, and if you talk to them they either don't respond or respond with great discomfort. It's hard or impossible to make eye contact with them, and it's very hard to engage them in play. The tension they feel is palpable; it fills the room.

With the relatively comfortable children the therapist can interact in an easy and natural manner. These children give plenty of clues about themselves. For instance, if you were to ask a question they weren't ready or willing to answer, chances are they would tell you they didn't want to talk about it. Now, with the uncomfortable children the clues are of a different order. With them you would get silence, avoidance of you and of the play materials, and a withdrawn and unhappy manner.

Generally, with the relatively comfortable children you get a pretty clear reading of how close you can come, and by that I mean how direct you can be about what brought them to treatment, what their feelings are about themselves and various family members, what their wishes, fantasies, and fears are, and so forth. I don't mean that you would choose to talk about all these things in the first session. I just mean that these things are readily assessable and might be talked about fairly soon in treatment.

When I refer to closeness I am thinking of how much our patients can and want to reveal their deepest feelings. With the more comfortable children the closeness factor will vary. Sometimes they will want to keep you far away and at other times they will want you close by, and you will need to be attuned to their communications and take care to respect them consistently.

Now, with the other group, the shy, withdrawn children, you will have to find your way in communicating with them without much obvious direction from them. Their silence and tension will be their primary clues, and you will have to invent a language to fit that. So what might you say to a child who comes for his first appointment looking sad and who sits down in a chair, stares into space, and acts as if you aren't in the room? You might say something like:

"I wonder whether you wish you weren't here, I do wonder that. You know, some children don't believe that coming to see me is going to help them feel more comfortable, but I'm going to try to figure out how to be helpful and often it works out well. We'll see. One thing we know so far is that the time of your appointments will be for you to use as you wish, and that means that you can be quiet and not talk to me, or talk about whatever interests you. You can use my toys or not use them, you can draw and write or not do either. How you spend your time here will be up to you. You will be the boss of your time here."

And you might or might not at some point in that first session also say to that child:

"Our time together is private. I will not discuss our time with anyone, not your parents or teachers, not with anyone. You don't have to talk about it either if you don't want to. If anyone asks you can tell them that it's private."

I'm a little more tentative about saying the second part, the part about privacy. If the child is very withdrawn it might sound too intimate, too "close." It might imply a partnership that doesn't exist yet. You'd have to give some thought to whether this child could tolerate the statement about the private nature of therapy. Yet the private nature of the therapy situation is very important and needs to be stated to a child early in treatment. With a very withdrawn child it might be enough to just say at the end of the session:

"I don't know whether you know this but if anyone asks you about what we did together, you don't have to tell them if you don't want to."

Or you might say:

"I told your mom and dad that therapy is private and that I can't talk to them about your time with me, and that you have the right to be private about it as well."

Although the notion of confidentiality has to be conveyed to the child at some point early in treatment, it has to be done with cautious attention to the fact that the "privacy" of the sessions represents separation and individuation, a state of apartness from the parents that might be too threatening for some children to tolerate.

QUESTION: I would like to be very clear about how we convey the purpose of treatment to children in all diagnostic groups. In the statement you made to a withdrawn and uncommunicative child I think the emphasis was on the nonintrusive nature of your role and possibly on the private aspect of treatment. Would you agree with that?

ANSWER: That was a big part of the example I gave of how one might verbalize the purpose and nature of treatment to a seemingly unwilling patient. But remember that I include the goal of treatment as making it possible for him to become more comfortable.

QUESTION: But it seemed that the unintrusive nature of your role was stressed more than the goal of arriving at greater comfort. Why the greater emphasis on the child's autonomy within the treatment situation, and your willingness to let him set the terms, and not the emphasis on his becoming a more comfortable human being?

ANSWER: Your question goes right to the heart of the matter. The withdrawn and very uncomfortable child might not have any idea of what a comfortable state is like. There are children whose regular anxiety levels are so high that they never or rarely experience a state of comfort. Their affective range might be limited to variations within levels of discomfort— between panic-level anxiety and less intense states of discomfort. To talk about comfort might be to talk about something they might not know and therefore cannot recognize. In that case *comfortable* would be a word empty of real meaning. That would not be productive. What we hope is that they will find a measure of comfort within the therapy situation, that they will eventually recognize this affective state, have a name for it, and remember that it exists, is desirable, and is within their reach.

So yes, given such a patient it is more productive to talk about the immediate situation, his therapy hour, as a time when you will respect his communications and stay at the distance he requires of you. With some children it's particularly useful to focus on the time and date of the appointments, on their unwavering regularity, their specific duration, in other words on the area that has to do with the inanimate aspects of treatment, to focus on the setting from the viewpoint of time, place, and duration. Now of course the setting involves the therapist and there is nothing inanimate about that, but with some children, placing the emphasis on the inanimate feels less threatening and that's helpful to them.

QUESTION: So in the way you introduce treatment you take into account the anxiety level of the child and allow that to guide your presentation?

ANSWER: Yes. *Being aware of the anxiety level of our patients, adults and children, is always of paramount importance. It's an essential barometer of the patient's moment-to-moment experience. When anxiety reaches very high intensity, the patient, of course, suffers terribly and will use any defense at his disposal to deal with his painful state. It's our job to be sensitive to fluctuations in our patients' anxiety states and not allow anxiety to reach overwhelming proportions.* We can't always succeed. Sometimes we fail in this regard and that's unfortunate because once a patient experiences panic-level or near-panic-level anxiety, he is generally out of our reach. When that happens the patient's sense of reality can become blurred and sometimes it can seem to the patient that his painful affect has been intentionally caused by the therapist or by the treatment situation. When this occurs, an adult might leave treatment and a child might beg his parents not to send him. So, as you can see, we do need to be very sensitive to the patient's anxiety level and to the fluctuations that occur during the session.

QUESTION: We're discussing a child's first therapy session and all of a sudden we're talking about overwhelming anxiety in a patient of any age. What is it about our field that causes us to slide so easily from one subject to another?

ANSWER: This sliding around, as you put it, is very typical in a field where linear thinking is not relevant. We never follow a straight path from A to B to C; it just doesn't work that way when people's emotions, unconscious fantasies, wishes, and fears are churned up by a process that explores their inner landscape. In our work everything relevant to being human is at play all the time, sometimes one aspect gaining prominence, sometimes another.

Being aware of a patient's anxiety is always very important, but during the initial period of treatment and especially during that first session, the importance cannot be overstressed.

QUESTION: Why is it particularly important during that first session?

ANSWER: Because if we're not aware of the patient's anxiety level we might say something that feels threatening to the patient, and depending how egregious our error, the patient might feel anywhere from somewhat offended and misunderstood to quite furious and wanting to leave and never return.

QUESTION: It sounds as if we can lose the patient if we make a serious error during that first session, but would you say the error would generally be in not being sensitive to the patient's anxiety level, or could there be other reasons for losing the patient in the first session? And how would we lose a child patient when it's the parents who decide whether or not to send him?

ANSWER: With an adult who has seen you several times in consultation and has voluntarily decided to work with you it would probably have to be a pretty big error that would cause him to leave at that point. It would not necessarily be lack of attunement to his anxiety level. It could be inflicting a narcissistic injury and not recognizing its effect on the patient. Let me give you an example.

Take as commonplace an incident as Mrs. M. arriving ten minutes late for her first appointment. She had already met with you three times during the consultation process and had arrived a little early for each of those appointments. On this, the date of her first regular session, she's late for the first time and visibly distressed about it. Talking to you in an agitated manner she tells you that her subway was stuck between stations for twenty minutes and therefore her lateness is no fault of hers. She says that she was very eager to come and has a lot to talk about, she needs her full session, and hopes that you will extend her hour to include the ten minutes she has missed. You tell her that you cannot do that and she gets very angry and tells you that that's unfair, she's being wrongly punished, she has no control over the subway, and how can you have such rigid and arbitrary rules. She becomes quite shrill and you hold your ground and retain a practical and logical tone. She leaves in a rage, calling you a rigid and unfeeling person, and tells you that she wouldn't dream of coming back. She never returns.

What would you say went wrong?

QUESTION: The therapist didn't address the patient's distress but instead stayed with the practical issue of making up the ten minutes. But how could the therapist have handled it better?

ANSWER: You've already answered your own question. You have the general idea but perhaps you need some help in implementing it. Let me begin by saying that a long time ago I had a wonderful teacher, Rubin Blanck, who stood in front of my class and said, "Patient is always right." I have found that to be a profoundly helpful statement. It has gotten me out of many difficult situations by helping me stop and try to grasp what might be happening to the patient, or between the patient and me, that had escaped my range of awareness. *Considering the idea that the patient is always right forces us to broaden our field of awareness at the very times that we might most need to, at times when our own thinking might be too concrete, too subject to our own agendas. Embracing this extraordinarily simple yet complex idea helps us maintain a professional attitude.*

In the above example it would have helped to acknowledge that yes, there is unfairness in a patient having to miss part of her session due to circumstances beyond her control. This acknowledgment might have conveyed concern for the patient's distress rather than just focusing on our therapy rules. It might have opened up paths of exploration about anxiety around lateness, about helplessness, and so forth. As it turned out, the patient's parting words were not without accuracy. The therapist was indeed unfeeling and rigid and had also underestimated the patient's narcissistic vulnerability.

QUESTION: Now we've slipped into talking about adults, and it's helpful, but what about a child's first session? What if the child wants to take home her drawings and we tell her that she has to leave them in the office in a special folder because that's a therapy rule and we have to stick to it? What if she starts screaming and crying and saying that we're unfair and hateful and she wants to go home right that minute and never come back? What if her mother knocks on the door and wants to know what's going on? What do we do then?

ANSWER: Even though we were talking about an adult a minute ago and now are switching to discussing a child, the principle of maintaining our professional attitude, which includes the idea that the patient is always right, still applies. So how, in practical terms, do we apply it to a screaming child and a mother banging on the door even though all that happened is that we said "no" to something the child wanted? Did I say that *all* we said was "no"? Evidently "no" is no small thing to this child, so we'd better look at that right away.

Remember Spitz's (1959) famous three organizers of the psyche: the smile at 3 months, stranger anxiety at 8 months, and the word "no" at 18 months. We know that the toddler's ability to use that word indicates a newly discovered state of separateness and autonomy. The aggressive drive can now be channeled to find expression in a word. Since the word is an abstraction, we are also witnessing the toddler's move into symbolic thinking. These mighty achievements are indicators that significant leaps in ego development have occurred, aided by the child's ability to identify with the "no"-saying parents.

In light of that brief review of a piece of developmental theory, are you better equipped to deal with the screaming child in your office and her upset mother banging on the door?

QUESTION: Yes, I think so, but in this imagined situation things are so out of hand that it's hard for me to think what to do with all the rumpus now that it's in full swing. Could we go back and talk about what to do now and also how it could have been avoided?

ANSWER: Let's begin by remembering that the information we gather during the evaluation process is key to our diagnostic formulation about our patients, both children and adults. In the case of the distraught girl and her equally upset mother, if we consider what we had learned about the child prior to that first session, could we have predicted great upset at being handed a "no"? If this turns out to be a complete surprise it might indicate that we failed to ask some important questions during the evaluation period when we were gathering information about the child.

QUESTION: Would you actually ask the parents whether their child has difficulty in being told "no"?

ANSWER: A broader question would yield richer information. For instance, I always ask parents how their children respond to daily routines. Do they come to meals when called? What is it like to put them to bed at night? Or if they're older, do they go to bed when told to? Do they get ready for school without too much prodding? Do they generally abide by the rules of the house? Each answer leads to another question. Pretty soon you have a pretty good idea of how your patient might respond to the very few but very firm rules of therapy.

Chances are that the nature of the referring problem, the child's history, and your observations combined to make such a strong reaction to your "no" pretty predictable. This is not a categorical statement, but it's likely that this child's reaction should not have come as a surprise.

QUESTION: Had I known to expect such upset at my "no," what would I have done when she reached to take home her pictures?

ANSWER: You would have anticipated that she might not be able to stand a "no" from you. You might have said something like this:

"I have to tell you about something important, but I think you might not like it very much. I'll be interested in hearing what you think of it, so here it is. Even though you make pictures here as you do at home and at school, when you do it here it's a little different. When you do it here it's part of our therapy work. So it's important that I always write the date on your picture, or you can write it. We keep them all in a folder, with the dates, and then once in a while we can look through them and remember together. For instance, we might some day remember that this was your first picture here in this office with me, and that when you painted it you were 5 years and 3 months old and we were just getting to know each other. And then we might remember that that yellow one was something you did two months later when you had just had your room painted yellow. . . . We need to keep all the pictures together in this folder because they are important to our work together. They tell a story about our time together."

If we can mobilize her attention so that she can hear the therapist speak this way, that might ease things for her. That would depend on her capacity to delay just enough to become interested in what's being described and perhaps a bit curious about this new adult who seems so interested in her.

Or you might approach it very differently, perhaps tell her that you were told by her mom and dad that there is a word she just hates and that's the word "no." Since she hates it so you want her to know that you will only use it if you absolutely have to, and you'll only have to sometimes to uphold the rules of therapy. The rules are few, but very important. Sessions always end when the time is up. Nothing in the office can be taken home except on the last day of therapy when anything she made can go home if she wants to take it with her. The office always has to look the same so everything gets put away before the session ends, and finally, the therapy office has to be a safe place for people and toys, a place where nothing and no one gets hurt. You can add that since she hates the word "no" so much, you will try never to use it without warning her in advance. That way she will be ready for it and it won't be a surprise. But if you forget to warn her, could she please remind you that you made a mistake?

If you have these rules about keeping "no" out of the room most of the time she might not mind it so much when it appears.

Then, at a later point in treatment, after you've proven yourself pretty reliable, you can tell her that it's quite interesting that she hates a word so much. It's something that the two of you could do some detective work on. The way things are right now, anyone who wants to upset her just has to say that word, and boom, she's upset. Wouldn't it be good if she could just ignore them, or say "no" to them? Like: "No, you can't bother me!"

QUESTION: I'm getting the sense of how to make use of what we know, to use it therapeutically rather than bypassing or dodging it. In talking so simply and directly to a child you not only deal with the issue, but you convey the essence of treatment.

ANSWER: Now I'm going to ask you a question. How would you define the essence of treatment?

QUESTION: Oh, I couldn't answer that. Not yet anyway. But I did recognize some shading of it when you spoke. Right now I'm happy to have a better sense of what we want to achieve during the first session. It's very much what you suggested at the beginning of this chapter. The therapist provides the setting, the child provides the content and sets the pace. The therapist joins the child and accepts whatever unfolds as important and meaningful. Slowly the child begins to understand that something new and different is being created, a special partnership. Would you agree?

ANSWER: Absolutely. *In the first session the therapist would like to convey that she is a useful and competent person who is there for the benefit of the child. Most children get a sense of the special nature of the relationship pretty fast.* Some take longer, and some don't stay in treatment long enough for the working alliance to really develop because they've been pulled out of treatment by their parents.

QUESTION: This is the longest we've discussed child treatment without mentioning the parents. I guess that's so because we've been talking about the child's first session. But I imagine that the child's first session has great meaning for the parents.

ANSWER: Yes, absolutely. Parents have many reactions to their child's first session. Sometimes they feel relief that help has been secured, but often that may combine with resentment that help was needed. They might feel a sense of accomplishment that they did what needed to be done, but also apprehension at what role the therapist will now play in the life of their child and in their lives. They might have positive feelings for the therapist or negative ones, or the parents might be in disagreement over the choice of therapist. The variations of responses are endless and in many cases these reactions to their child's treatment undergo many changes. The therapist will need to be aware of these varying affective states in the parents and respond with sensitivity and wisdom.

8

৵৽

Management Problems in the Treatment of Children

QUESTION: There are so many difficulties that arise in just managing a session with certain children that it's hard to feel as if any therapeutic gains can take place. For instance, some children are so restless and destructive that it's hard to just get through a session without the office being wrecked and the therapist becoming frazzled and exhausted. What can we do to contain some of these very difficult young patients?

ANSWER: Some children exhibit behavior that's hard to contain for many reasons. It makes our job somewhat easier if we know what lies beneath the kind of out-of-bounds behavior you're describing. Are we dealing with a psychotic child who lives in a panic state and is unable to feel safe or comfortable, or are we dealing with a child whose impulse control is very poor, or is this a child who is oppositional and defiant . . . and so forth.

QUESTION: In what ways would knowing all that make us control difficult behavior more effectively?

ANSWER: Diagnostic understanding of our patients always helps us in our work. I don't mean the kind of diagnostic labeling required by insurance companies. That does nothing to inform the therapist. I refer here to diagnostic understanding that gives us insight into the patient, into how he experiences his world, his surroundings, his sense of self, and his perception of other people. I refer to a level of understanding that really informs the therapist and provides vital information about the patient, including insight into his grip on reality, his defensive system, his anxiety level, and his adaptive capacities.

When we do a good job of gaining information from the parents during the initial interviews, and of paying attention to the presented problem, we learn a lot about the child in advance of seeing him, and we also learn what kinds of questions to ask the parents to further illuminate a picture of the child. This process never ends; it continues throughout treatment. The more we learn about a child, the more we know what to ask his parents about him as the treatment process moves ahead. In some cases, we might supplement information gained from collateral sources during the evaluation process by again contacting some of these people in the child's life: teachers, guidance counselors, the referring person, and so forth.

When prior to seeing the child we learn that he exhibits wild, destructive, or unpredictable behavior, it makes sense to find out what approach has been found effective in helping him control himself. It's equally useful to ask what types of situations trigger out-of-control behavior. If the parents are constantly baffled by what sets their child off, and also by what soothes him, this in itself is diagnostically significant, and I would take it to suggest the possibility that we were going to find the presence of severe pathology. Parents usually know what triggers and what soothes their child. When they don't know, when they are perpetually baffled by their child, either they are incredibly unattuned or the child might be very disturbed, possibly psychotic.

QUESTION: Suppose a child has been referred by his school because he hits other children, won't stay in his seat, and yells out instead of raising his hand. Suppose this is the presenting problem. What kind of information would you gather in order to feel that you would be able to contain him in your office?

ANSWER: The information you have so far is just enough to alert you that this child might be difficult to contain. But here it's important not to jump to conclusions, since many children who have difficulty in a group situation do very well in the one-to-one situation of a therapy session.

Let's go back to the example of a child who has so much difficulty at school that it leads to a referral for treatment. Here we would have good reason to wonder whether it might be equally difficult to contain him in a therapy session or whether it was the group situation, or the teacher, or some other factor that was particularly difficult for him. We would immediately be on much firmer ground if we learned as much as possible about this child prior to seeing him.

Naturally we would need to know his age, what kind of a school he's in, whether what he yells out in class is some sort of gibberish, or the right answer to a question the teacher asked. You see, it makes a big difference to know that a child is 6 years old, in a regular school with well-developing kids, and that what he yells out is the correct answer, rather than 12 years old, in a special school for children who are emotionally or educationally impaired, and what he yells out are primary process phrases that have no bearing on whatever is going on in the real world. I'm using extremes to make my point. But I think you would agree that it would make a big difference to have this information before seeing this child for the first time.

QUESTION: I would agree. To begin with I would feel less intimidated by the 6-year-old than by the 12-year-old. The 12-year-old is bigger and much more disturbed. If he became violent I would be scared, and that would be bad for both of us. I don't think I would be scared of a feisty 6-year-old, and by not being scared I would be better able to maintain my role as the adult in charge. But let's go on with this approach. What else can you say that would enable the therapist to best prepare for seeing either of these children?

ANSWER: You made the observation that it's important that the therapist not feel scared of the child. That's a very valuable observation and a very honest perspective to take. If the therapist is afraid it undermines her professional effectiveness. The therapist needs to feel confident, in command, and therefore able to concentrate on the patient and the work at hand. So, to answer your question about preparing to see a child whose presenting problem is that he goes out of control, I would suggest you use your comfort level as a guide. You find out what sorts of situations upset him and what calms him. You find out what kinds of materials he likes to use and have them ready. You make sure the parent who brings him will be there for the entire time, either in the waiting room or in your office with you and the patient. Also, if you see that things are getting seriously out of hand, you don't hesitate to end the session at that point, even if you haven't used up the allotted time.

I want to add another cautionary note. It's important not to take a case on until you've assessed your ability to deal with the situation. That means that when you begin an evaluation you are evaluating a total situation, which includes information and observations about the child and his parents and also includes your assessment of your ability and willingness to work with them and give them the time and attention they need. You would best serve everyone, the parents, the child, the referring person, and yourself, if at the beginning you make it known that you will assess the total situation, and see what needs to be done, and that will include your role in the child's treatment, if it's to take place. You make it clear that if you are not the right person to treat their child, you will find a therapist more suited to working with him.

Should you find that the pathology is extreme and you feel daunted by the child's state of panic and disorganization, you would do him no favor by taking him on. Some of us are more capable of dealing with extreme pathology than others. Those who are less comfortable in this area should accept this about themselves and rely on those who are less daunted by this aspect of the work. I don't mean that this need remain so forever. Some of us change in what we're able to deal with professionally. This is not a matter of experience and knowledge. Some very inexperienced therapists are able to work with extreme pathology and continue to do well in this area of work throughout their careers. Others grow into that ability while still others lose their initial aptitude or interest in this area of work and no longer take it on as they grow older and more experienced. Perhaps energy levels have some bearing on this. I'm not sure. But if you feel you really aren't up to coping with a child who hits and bites and shouts to hallucinatory images, don't take the case on. Of course in some agency settings the therapists might not have much choice in the matter. If you find yourself drafted into doing work that feels intimidating, I recommend getting as much supervisory help as possible, even if you have to go beyond your agency setting and pay for it out of pocket.

QUESTION: It's very important to remember that we usually don't have to take on a case that scares us. But what happens if the parents eagerly ask you to treat their child and you discover during the evaluation process that the situation is too much for you?

ANSWER: Sometimes it's very difficult to turn parents down, particularly if you've made a good connection with them and they really like you and want you to treat their child. It can be very hard to say "no" to them and cause them to feel rejected. But if you feel it would require more energy than you possess, they need to know that it would be in their best interest to have their child work with someone who has the energy and stamina the situation requires.

Every once in a while I've found myself unwilling to take on a case for a variety of reasons. Sometimes I find the parents very difficult from the first moment of contact on the telephone. If their manner is belligerent and they demand conditions that are not acceptable to me, I simply tell them that I'm not available. That's not a particularly difficult situation. However, sometimes the parents sound fine but what they describe about their child makes me uneasy about taking the case on in my private office in a quiet residential building where it's important that my patients not create a disturbance. When I feel that my office setup doesn't fit the situation, I don't go on to do a full evaluation but tell the parents at that first interview that I'm not the right therapist for their child. I try to explain by combining tact and forthrightness in the hope of serving everyone's best interest.

Some children need to be seen in an agency setting where noisy disruptive behavior in the waiting room and loud scenes during and at the end of sessions are a natural occurrence, and where experienced receptionists and other staff members can step in and lend a hand as difficulties arise. I was recently told by a supervisee that he had to call a security guard to help stop a 12-year-old boy who was banging his head against the wall and not letting his therapist near him. It took the full combined strength of the therapist and security guard to stop this boy's self-destructive behavior. Luckily the agency had a security guard on hand.

If it seems likely that a child is going to be very disruptive and physically hard to contain, the parents might need to be told that their child's needs would be better served in an agency setting that offers the services of a broader spectrum of professionals. Besides the availability of the non-professional staff, agencies have psychologists and psychiatrists on hand, should psychological tests and medication or even arrangements for hospitalization be needed. These professionals are available to work cooperatively with the therapist during both the evaluation and the treatment process. Thus they can step in if needed when the therapist is on vacation or out ill. They know the case and are usually familiar with the child and have records available to them. The fact that they work in a setting familiar to the child is a decided advantage, should their help be needed in the therapist's absence. I am not suggesting that the therapist is interchangeable with other professionals. Not at all. But at least these people are not total strangers and that's a decided advantage in an emergency.

QUESTION: What if you don't know that the child is given to terrible tantrums and violent outbursts? What if the first of these occurs three months into treatment and takes you by surprise? What if these then occur frequently? What if the child refuses to leave at session's end, holds on to the legs of your couch and will not let go, and screams if you try to go near him, and his noise reaches your waiting room where your next patient is exposed to hearing all this as he is kept waiting week after week? What do you do then?

ANSWER: That's a really tough situation and not one you can allow to continue week after week. You can't sacrifice your next patient that way, or your peace of mind, nor can you

neglect the patient who is causing the disturbance by allowing him to continue to be such a nuisance. You would have
to put a stop to this behavior.

You would have to let this young patient know that his
behavior will not be tolerated. You would have to tell him
this at the beginning of his session, or at least at a time when
he was relatively calm and able to hear you. You could begin by telling him that he had been getting very upset during his sessions. Then you could ask him whether he could
think of anything that would help him when he was just
beginning to get upset, something that would help him stop
the upset from getting so big. During this discussion you
would not let him ignore you or pick up his favorite toy and
shut you out. You would make it clear that this was an emergency and you had to impose the subject of discussion. You
might even remind him that one of the principles of his time
with you is that he always gets to decide how he will spend
his time. You could say that this was such a big emergency
that you are changing this important rule in order to take
care of the emergency. If he still ignored you, you would tell
him that since he is not helping to solve the problem you
will have to do it alone and this is what you're going to do.
Since ending his sessions requires so much time you will
end them earlier.

You decide on a new length for his sessions, leaving a lot
of time between the end of his session and that of the next
patient. You let him know that changing the length of his
sessions is another sign of what a big emergency this is since
the length of sessions is always supposed to be forty-five
minutes. In addition, you do not let his parent or baby-sitter leave the waiting room to do errands. The person who
brings him must sit there for the whole time. You tell him
this and also that he will have his full time back when he's
able to use words and play to say what he wants to say and
is able to leave when his time is up. You can add that you
can't do your work as a therapist unless he agrees to do as

you say. You can remind him that you are the "boss" of making your office and time together safe and helpful. After a certain number of times of ending the sessions say, twenty minutes earlier than the forty-five minutes, you can add five minutes to his time, but only if the sessions resume a more manageable tone. You would, of course, tell him that you are adding five minutes to his time and why. You could continue to add five-minute increments until he has his full time back.

You asked for an approach that might work in a particular situation so I made this up on the spur of the moment. I've never had to do anything this drastic myself, although I've treated children who refused to leave and created a disturbance, which caused their time to run into that of the following patient. Usually taking a very strong stand and shortening their sessions once or twice was enough to remedy the situation.

Perhaps the more drastic approach I came up with sounds like a behavior modification technique, which is really not my orientation, so let me clarify what I had in mind. My objective is to protect him, the next patient, and myself from his out-of-control behavior. I came up with a solution that rested on two principles. The first was to help him become more aware of the beginning of his out-of-control behavior, to try to identify it, and mobilize *inner* resources to regulate it. The second was to position myself as the "boss" of the therapy situation, and in that capacity demand that he meet my expectations for behavior that would allow us to do our work. This twofold approach is based on psychoanalytic developmental theory insofar as it takes into account the development of self-regulation. The young child identifies with parental strength, which provides order, structure, and safety. Through the processes of identification the child is gradually able to take over some parental function and develop self-regulation. When that happens, the child can reflect and talk rather than discharge affects into action. So you see, this is not at all behavior modification. This is psychoanalytic developmental theory applied to acting-out behavior.

Now I grant you there must be other ways of conveying the objective of more manageable sessions that end on time. The approach I just presented is but one of many possibilities. Once you are clear about the principle of this communication, you can present your version of it in a variety of ways. The principle is that *you, the therapist, are the boss of the therapy situation, and that pertains to time, place, noise level, safety, care of equipment, and care of the people in the therapy room, the waiting room, and the entire therapy suite. Implicit in this principle is the goal of helping the child become the boss of his affects and behavior, a person who can think and talk instead of just acting out.*

QUESTION: Would you say that the principle about the therapist being the boss of therapy applies equally to the parents? That with them as well, you are the boss of the therapy situation?

ANSWER: Absolutely, yes.

QUESTION: But when you present a plan for the treatment of a child to his parents, what if they can't bring him as often as you suggest, or the parents can't see you as often as you feel would be optimal, or are unable to stay in the waiting room while you see their child because they have errands to do during that time, or other such complications? Do you not bend at all?

ANSWER: The question was whether the therapist is the boss of the therapy situation. My answer was a resounding yes. Does that mean that under some circumstances I might accept less than ideal frequency of appointments? Sure, but only under some circumstances. Would I accept parents leaving their young child with me while they went out and did some errands during the child's appointment? Yes, of course. This is in fact what commonly happens once a child is comfortable at having the parents go off this way. But would I allow that with parents who are late in picking their child up, upset their child, disrupt my time with the patient that follows, and ruffle my concentration? No. Those parents would have to stay in the waiting room. I would give them no choice there.

Let's remember that we opened this conversation with your question about how to manage hard-to-contain children. The most important issue here is this: we have to convey that we're strong, strong enough to be in charge no matter what happens. Our strength is essential to their sense of safety; the two are linked, indivisible. If you deeply believe this as fact, as I do, it's not so difficult to make certain strict rules, and to be "bossy" when that seems indicated.

Let me give you a clinical example that illustrates the importance of the therapist being strong and fully in charge. I once treated a psychotic child who lived in a state of panic. After a year of treatment (he was now 5), we had a fifteen-minute battle over whether he could take home one of my crayons. No matter how much he "needed it" and "had to have it" I would not relent. Finally he said to me:

> "I know you never let anything leave this office because you like me to always find everything looking the same. . . . when I want to take something home you always say 'no,' always, always, always. You're like a traffic light, green is always walk and red is always stop. I wish you were on every corner."

This was a child who had tantrums whenever his mother said "no" to him. The tantrums were so severe that his mother often said "yes" just to placate him, hoping he would forget whatever he had asked for. She lived in terror of his tantrums and of her retaliatory rage. My firmness with him was a source of wonder to her, and eventually she was able to identify with it and be less afraid of him, but this could only happen once she was able to experience more modulated affects towards him. This child had been her flawed baby, a wild unruly child who evoked her fiercest love and most desperate shameful hate.

My firmness with this mother was an essential and steadying component for her, a factor that enriched the working alliance. I was uncompromising about the frequency of sessions and about her presence in the waiting room. I was also completely available to her by telephone and understood her frequent phone calls (early in treatment as much as three in one day) as her desperate attempt to deflect her overwhelming frustration and accompanying rages at this child who could, in a couple of impulse-ridden seconds, cause a flood, a fire, or other damage of enormous proportions. These phone calls grew shorter with time. They also assumed their special shorthand. She'd call and in tears and say, "I'm going to kill him!"

I would ask, "What did he do?"

She would answer, "Knocked down a stack of dishes, my best china, because I told him they were for a grown-up party, no children invited. He went wild."

I would reply, "Where is he now?"

She would answer, "In his room, hiding from me . . . it's all right. I'm better already. I'll tell him that I'm still mad and sad but I'll be better soon. I'll tell him that."

"Wait," I would say, sensing that she was ready to hang up.

"Can you be more specific than soon?"

"Thank you," she would answer. "He doesn't tolerate 'soon' . . . I'll say I won't be so angry by the time *Sesame Street* comes on, and I won't be angry at all when I kiss him goodnight."

That's all it took of my time to help her regain her equilibrium in this, her son's second year of treatment. A year or so later, she could usually have this conversation with me in her head. So this is an example of being very firm with a parent in one area and very liberal in another, in my availability to her when she felt unequal to dealing with her child.

QUESTION: How did you know she wouldn't exploit your availability and call you a lot when it wasn't an emergency?

ANSWER: I'm really glad you asked that question. At the time I was treating this child I worked for an agency and came under some criticism for being so available to this mother by telephone. I was told I was fostering her dependency on me rather than helping her become more independent in her dealings with her son. As it turned out my critic was wrong and I was correct in my approach, but that doesn't mean it might not have gone the other way. If it had, if this mother had called me about what on the surface were trivial matters, whether her son should wear a blue or a green shirt, brush his teeth before or after his bedtime story, and so forth, I would have wondered what was going on and called her in for a session with me. I would have tried to understand what she was looking for, perhaps helped her discover and articulate some need or concern she could not identify or express, a need that took an unfortunate cloak, one of insignificance. Together we might have come up with something helpful, that made sense, and allowed her to ask for what she really needed.

As therapists we have to be careful not to fall into popular clichés and talk about fostering dependency in our patients. The therapeutic relationship is far too complex to be reduced to such a simple idea. Of course there are situations wherein it appears that a therapist is promoting her patient's dependency, but is that the most insightful way of conceptualizing a situation where one person is fostering another to need her, lean on her, and feel lost without her? It would be more accurate to say that if a therapist were to be engaged in promoting such behavior, there would be a serious countertransferential enactment in progress, and it would be overriding everything else that was going on in that person's treatment. This type of enactment could take place with any adult or child, or with the parent of a child in treatment. When this sort of thing happens, its origin is unconscious; the therapist might be unaware of what's happening in response to her patient.

It is of great importance not to confuse and lump together interventions and behaviors that might superficially look alike but are really very different in origin and purpose. For instance, being kind to a patient is not the same as overgratifying him. Kindness is a human attribute that is to varying degrees part of one's character. It hasn't been studied very much in our profession, but I can safely say that it is not to be confused with disregarding the abstinence rule (Freud 1915) *and gratifying our patients' id wishes or even their demands for narcissistic enhancement. Being kind is not going to promote dependency* any more than being interested and curious might. If a patient has strong dependency needs they will eventually emerge and we will welcome them. How else are we going to address them if they remain hidden behind super self-sufficiency, arrogance, entitlement, or any other attribute whose purpose is to defend against such needs?

QUESTION: But sometimes parents do call with inappropriate demands, and if we continually meet these demands, aren't we going off course?

ANSWER: Yes, we are. We're not addressing the nature of these demands. If a parent calls and tells me she can't bring Judy to her session because Judy is dying to see a movie that goes on at the same hour as her appointment, we tell that parent we'd better sit down and talk about her request. We would be very much remiss if we simply granted the request. In fact, wouldn't we be treating Judy's mother the same way as Judy's mother proposes treating her? And we would be accepting a role of secondary importance. The difficulty here is in maintaining a professional attitude about the matter and not getting personally wounded by being given such low status.

QUESTION: As so often happens, we began talking about how to manage *children* who are hard to contain, and we ended up talking about how to deal with their parents. Perhaps that happens because we always have to deal with both and I think the principle of how we deal with either is the same. What it comes down to is that we have to maintain our professional perspective no matter what the situation. Could you say a little more about that?

ANSWER: I agree that maintaining our professional attitude is key in all these situations that on the surface appear practical, that seem to operate in an area beyond therapy, in a realm that seems more concrete and ordinary. I grant you that when a child has grabbed hold of our table leg and is holding on with all her might and refuses to let go, and her time is up and the office is a mess and the next patient is waiting and the child's mother hasn't returned to the waiting room from her errands, it's hard to think like a therapist. On the other hand, the knowledge we have as therapists and our power to observe and put our observations into words are the main things we have going for us. So we'd better harness that knowledge and capacity for insight and use it to deal with these situations, view the difficulty as a therapeutic challenge, and not relegate it to being a *practical* problem.

If I found myself in that situation, and once or twice I have, I would first wonder why I allowed that mother to go off and do errands during her child's hour, knowing that she wasn't the most punctual person and that her child had trouble leaving at session's end. Then I would wonder why

I scheduled the next patient so close to the end of this child's appointment. Knowing that a child is very demanding and has trouble leaving her session, even if the ending of sessions became manageable, why would I not give myself a few minutes in between sessions to gather my thoughts and have some quiet before the next appointment? These are not practical questions. They have a practical component, but they're questions directed at countertransferential issues. If I allow the mother to go off and do errands because she's so cranky and unpleasant whenever I don't yield to her wishes, I'm saying yes because I'm afraid to say no. Then I have to figure out who she represents and what I'm enacting with her.

I have to do some similar self-reflecting regarding the child. How come I allowed this particular child to turn my office into such a mess? How come I allowed it knowing that this child will not help me clean up but will instead lie down on the floor and pretend to take a nap, or on bad days grab hold of the desk leg and refuse to leave? I know that with some children having every toy out and in use has a quality of time well spent, of energies invested, and of richness, and then putting everything back can in turn feel good and generate a spirit of mutuality of purpose. I also know that at the other extreme some children want to make a random mess because they don't know how else to make their presence felt and for them putting things away would feel annihilating, as if their tracks in the sand were erased by wind. Well of course those children are not going to help with the clean-up effort.

What I'm saying is that we have to think and learn and finally understand what we're being told by all this behavior. Then we might not let the more primitive messing go on too long. When we approach this sort of situation as therapists we try to take it as a communication, and when the communication fails to reach us, when we don't "get it," we have to say so to the child. We have to tell that child:

"Here you're showing me something, telling me with these toys, with your not talking to me, telling me something that I can't understand. I wish I did, I want to. Can you tell me another way? Well, even if you can't right now, I'll get to understand after a while, and it might get easier to tell me when we get to know each other better."

But at the same time you remind the child of your purpose in her life you can also say to that child:

"From now on I'm not going to let you take everything in the toy cabinet and throw it all over the office. Putting it back is not something you want to do and it's too much for me to do alone. So from now on you can take out half of the toys, two shelves instead of four. Then I'll have time to put them away while we're together. It will make it easier to say goodbye at the end of your time. Someday you might get to want to put things back, and then we'll work together and we'll have time to put all four shelves back if you want that. We're learning to make your time with me a helpful time for you."

Most children would eventually understand that the therapy hour was not like any other time and that it was really an offering *for them.*

QUESTION: But what about a child refusing to clean up at the end of a session? Do you have rules about that?

ANSWER: Yes and no. I would not let it go unmentioned but I would not force a child to clean up. I have a prejudice against that phrase and never use it with children. It sounds to me as if the play materials that during the course of the session were removed from their shelves and used for play and communication are being referred to as a mess that needs to be cleaned away. Now maybe I'm being too literal to hear the phrase that way, but I do. I prefer to refer to the action of restoring the room to the way it looked at the beginning of the session as "putting everything back," or "putting away our things." I do not require children to do that if they don't want to. I do it in their presence and wonder out loud why they want me to do it alone, why they don't want us to do it together.

Often my question draws silence. Some children just tell me they don't want to, don't like it, hate to do it at home so why should they do it here. But I've also gotten some other interesting answers, the most common one being: "That's maid's work." When you hear such words from a young child, or even a child of any age, it's hard not to wonder what you're being told. It certainly opens up avenues to explore. Whatever they tell you is something that can be made use of, but not always right away.

QUESTION: Why don't you require children to put back what they've used during their hour? You have certain rules that you believe in. Why haven't you made this into a rule?

ANSWER: My rules have a common theme: safety and predictability. Whether I insist on ending sessions on time, not letting them take home therapy supplies or things they've made during the therapy hour, not letting them hurt or destroy any of my office furnishings, or in any way behave in a dangerous way regarding their body or mine, the theme is consistent. Putting back toys at the end of the session does not fit this theme so I don't enforce it. What I do enforce is that the putting away be done during their time, and of course I have to end the session a couple of minutes earlier if the room needs a lot of putting away and I am to do it alone.

Besides not regarding the putting back of toys as something children must do, there's also a very practical component to my not making this a rule. It would be a very difficult rule to enforce with some children and that would make the therapist look ineffectual and probably frighten children whose hostile, rebellious feelings were expressed in their refusal of this task. We would resemble the ineffectual parent who places himself vis-à-vis the child in such a way that one or the other is going to lose face.

We cannot afford to get into power struggles with our patients, adults or children. When situations arise that might take this destructive turn we have to examine them carefully. In our work we always have to look at things a little differently than in the rest of life. When we do that, we maintain our professional attitude by engaging our "work ego,"[9] no matter what the situation, and in so doing deepen the treatment and strengthen the working alliance.

---

9. This phrase was coined by Robert Fliess (1942) who used it in a somewhat different way than my use of it in this context.

9

ᔆ

Some Typical Dilemmas
in Work with Children

QUESTION: Sometimes a child wants to sit on his therapist's lap or wants the therapist to hug him or give him a kiss. This is particularly true of young children. What do you suggest doing in these situations?

ANSWER: Let's try to understand your question. You're obviously unsure about something, so could you explain what your dilemma is about?

QUESTION: Kissing, hugging, and holding a child on one's lap are very natural in the world outside the therapy office. These are usually kindly, affectionate, loving acts. I'm not sure they have a place in the office of a therapist. I'm not sure of their appropriateness between therapist and patient, even when the patient is a young child. Also, I'm a little afraid of gratifying a child in this way from the point of view of raising any suspicion in the parents that something improper is going on during the therapy hour. So my dilemma is that it seems hard to refuse to gratify these requests without causing our young patients to feel rejected, yet to gratify them is risky in more ways than one. What do I do when faced with a 4-year-old child who just climbs into my lap?

ANSWER: This is a very important question. Let's take our time with it and find a way to think about it that's helpful in a broad conceptual way. If we reflect on this in a way that's well grounded in our training, a way that considers sound and basic principles of treatment, we'll learn a lot. Let's begin with a specific situation and then move to applying what it teaches us to a broad spectrum of situations.

Do you actually have a 4-year-old who climbed into your lap during a session?

QUESTION: Yes. Kevin is 4 and he's a sweet, shy little boy whose language development is on the slow side. I had him tested and he's of average intelligence, but his ability to concentrate is very limited and he seems very young in his play, in his interest in the world, and in his ability to communicate. His teachers don't think he's going to be ready for kindergarten next year. That got his parents so upset they decided to seek professional help in the hope that a therapist would identify and understand the basis of what they called "his deficits," and find a way to help him, and at the same time help them understand him so they could help him at home. These parents are ambitious and high achieving, and their dreamy, affectionate little boy both delights and disturbs them.

ANSWER: What's it like to be with Kevin?

QUESTION: Well, I just started working with him. I've seen him three times in all. I'm considering this an extended consultation because I haven't decided for sure that treatment is the right course of action for him. He's a little bland and a little immature. He's not a high-IQ child, at least at the current testing. So when very bright parents have a child who seems closer to average, is that a reason for treatment? You can see I'm confused. What am I treating? Parental disappointment?

ANSWER: I can hear your confusion, and I've noticed that you didn't really answer my question about what it's like to be with Kevin. Also, I think you're expressing a bit of resentment but I'm not sure about what. Am I right?

QUESTION: Yes. It upsets me that the parents see this lovely child as flawed. Does everyone have to have a superior IQ to be considered okay?

ANSWER: Very bright parents generally expect their children to be very bright. That's a fact of life. I'm afraid you're going to have to accept it as such or you're going to be at odds with many parents.

Okay, now the picture is rounding out for me. You're in the process of doing an extended evaluation of a little boy whose parents are concerned and perhaps disappointed that he isn't more verbal and intellectually advanced. The little boy doesn't seem unhappy or tense but he doesn't seem particularly invested in the world around him. He's a friendly child who, when he comes to your office, doesn't talk much or explore your office and toys, but rather seeks physical contact with you. Is seeking physical contact his primary way of communicating and making contact with another person? Do you know whether this is his general mode with other adults, and/or with children?

QUESTION: Yes, the parents reported that he was a cuddly baby and that he hasn't changed in this regard. He continues to be very affectionate with everyone. In fact the parents were concerned that he's so indiscriminate in this regard that he would go up to strangers in the playground and climb into their laps if they let him.

ANSWER: Let's try to round out the overall picture so far and also try to conceptualize it. When Kevin tries to climb into your lap you see him as an affectionate little boy whose verbal ability seems limited and who's trying to make contact with you the best way he can. But you also recognize that he's a 4-year-old child whose way of making contact is fairly primitive and whose object connections are perhaps lacking in specificity; in other words, they're indiscriminate. Now if that's the case, his parents are not just intellectual snobs. They have a child who warrants some concern. After all, we do expect a 4-year-old to reserve judgment with strangers, to not be so ready to express affection or to seek physical contact with unfamiliar adults, or to accept their overtures. We expect a 4-year-old to be able to use speech and play for the purpose of communication and in feeling out a new situation.

QUESTION: Well, that's a more accurate picture of Kevin than the one I presented. So with this view of the lag between Kevin and a 4-year-old whose development follows a more usual path, how would you handle his climbing into my lap?

ANSWER: If we accept the possibility that there might be a developmental lag, what would you be doing by letting him climb into your lap? As you see, I want you to figure this out. I think something is getting in your way, blocking your understanding of this situation.

QUESTION: You're probably right. I'm having trouble admitting that something could be wrong with Kevin. It's much easier for me to feel that his parents are snobs, that his teachers are too fussy about not very important developmental milestones, and that our whole society sets too many standards of behavior and achievement and doesn't sufficiently respect individual differences and the uniqueness of each person, adult or child.

ANSWER: All you say about the parents, the teachers, and society is probably true. But why is that easier to accept than the possibility of something being amiss with Kevin?

QUESTION: He's a cute, wide-eyed little boy with an ingenuous smile. I don't want anything to be wrong with him. I'm not being rational. I'm being emotional and not very professional. Yet I can't shake my reluctance to see this child diagnostically and deal with whatever deficits are there.

ANSWER: You're not alone in having difficulty forming an objective assessment of childhood pathology. It's a common failing among child therapists, a countertransferential enactment that we all play out at one time or another. Just look at how it plays out in the case of Kevin. For some reason you're so identified with this child that you're going to take on the world. You are his defender and champion. Anyone who thinks there's something wrong with Kevin is the enemy. You are his only ally.

We've talked before about this most common form of countertransference in child treatment: the therapist over-identifies with her young patient and enacts a rescue fantasy. This is destructive on many many counts and is an obstacle to getting any therapeutic work done. *This child, like all young patients, does need your help, but he needs your help as a therapist. He does not need you to try to become a better parent than the other adults in his life. He needs you to help him communicate in a way that has some fullness and*

the means to reach out to a wider, more interesting world. The climbing into the lap was transformed from problem for the therapist to symptom of the child's stuckness.

I think we got a lot out of your question. I believe you were wondering how the "abstinence rule" (Freud 1915) applies to child treatment. I think you must have concluded that to a large degree it applies, that to simply and automatically gratify Kevin's wish to sit in your lap is as counterproductive as any other unexamined response to the wish of a patient. You were at first distracted by your countertransference, but once we addressed its presence you found a way of getting him off your lap and into treatment.

There was another issue that complicated the situation: the fear that you might be accused of improper conduct for having physical contact with Kevin. That fear has to be taken very seriously because we do live in a litigious society and you do have to protect yourself from possible accusations of misconduct. So with that in mind, it's wise to really get to know the parents of your young patients, to learn from them something about their children's habits and needs regarding physical contact, and the parents' reaction to this general subject. If relevant, it could be useful to let the parents know something about your attitude about physical contact and care in the therapy situation. Sometimes, for instance, a parent goes off to do errands during the child's hour and the child, age 3, needs to use the toilet and wants you to wipe him. Do you tell him to wipe himself, do you oblige, or do you ask the parent to stick around during subsequent sessions so as to be available should this situation arise?

QUESTION: We're taking the position that physical intimacy is questionable even with very young children. Is this a position that would find consensus among therapists?

ANSWER: Probably many would agree, but there would be quite a few therapists who think differently and who would not agree with us. But then their basic principles of treatment might be different from ours. I have heard child therapists talk about inducing a regressive state in a child so as to be able to give the child the chance to relive and work through an early trauma. This is not my therapeutic territory but it's the way some people work. They would not agree with our position on this subject.

One more point about Kevin before we move on. Now that we've reached an approach that makes sense to both of us, can you go back a bit and try to understand why you avoided answering my question about what it was like to be with him?

QUESTION: I think so. You see, it's been kind of dull to be with him. He's adorable and has a ready smile and big beautiful blue eyes, but I never quite know what to do with him because he doesn't respond much to my attempts to engage him or to my toys. He seems content to just look around, or lean against me, or try to sit in my lap, and then I feel kind of bored and helpless and lost. I now see that I didn't like being with him all that much, and I couldn't bear to admit it. So I criticized his parents and teachers and got theoretical about our society's overemphasis on high intelligence.

ANSWER: Your response of feeling somewhat bored and helpless is a red flag, a valuable diagnostic alarm signal. Probably more than anything you were told by the parents and teachers, your visceral response to Kevin gave you information of great value about him. But the information was very disturbing because this very cute and friendly little boy seems very bland and unable to communicate and connect except on the very primitive level of body contact. You were so disturbed by what it was like to be with him that you disavowed it rather than making use of it, as you did later when you realized what was happening and devised ways to engage him.

I think we've done a lot with your case example, so let's move on to other issues particular to child treatment. But before we leave Kevin I do want to focus on something that came out of that discussion.

When the therapist is bored, distracted, daydreaming, or disengaged from his patient in whatever way, this is not something to ignore. This is an indication of something amiss in the treatment situation on many levels. The case cannot move on until this hurdle is understood and eliminated.

QUESTION: But some children play with their back toward you, act as if you aren't there, talk to themselves inaudibly, or do boring repetitive games with cars or dolls and seem to want no part of you.

ANSWER: When a child's session consists of noncommunication with the therapist, this then becomes the child's most compelling message. Perhaps not communicating is the only way he can convey his sense of isolation, his loneliness, his need for distance, and his fear of human exchange. If he's behaving as if you aren't there, that has to be recognized, made use of, stated, placed in the room as an important presence. This can be very difficult, since a child who seeks such distance might give few clues and really dread and fear being noticed and spoken to. On the other hand, the therapist would be remiss to accept the state of boredom and suffer out the hour. Sometimes when I find myself in a situation like that, I talk to myself out loud. I say things like:

> "Today Mary is playing with the doll she seems to pick every time she comes to see me, and today, as usual, she's putting that doll to sleep. I wonder why Mary always likes to do that? Or maybe she really doesn't like to do that but is doing it to show me something. But if that's it, what could it be? Oh dear, I wish I knew, but I can't read minds so I'll have to wait until Mary wants to tell me. . . ."

I don't think it matters terribly what I say as long as it's not too intrusive or too fantastic. With some children, just having the therapist show that much life and interest is worth something. It also helps the therapist stay more engaged by paying that kind of attention and summoning that much energy. Just the act of talking in this way utilizes ego functions that help the therapist stay focused and available.

QUESTION: That's helpful. Sometimes I get so sleepy and resentful when I can find no way in. But of course, the fact that the child is so distant and aloof is the problem.
Another issue that comes up for me is what to do about food during sessions. That seems like a similar kind of problem to letting a child sit in your lap. I know some child therapists offer their young patients snacks. I've not done that but some of my colleagues have pointed out that some children come right after school and really need a snack.

ANSWER: What do you find similar about providing food and providing a lap or a hug?

QUESTION: Well, in both cases it's providing a caretaking function, it's being parental. In neither case does it have much to do with our training or the primary role we play in the lives of our patients. Yet, don't you think it's kind of cold and unfeeling to have a hungry child in our office and not feed him?

ANSWER: No, I don't think it's necessarily unfeeling. I think it's an opportunity to find out why our young patient is hungry. Why didn't he tell his mother or father or whoever brings him that he's hungry and needs a snack before his appointment? Why didn't the parent or caretaker think of the child's state of hunger after a long day of school? This is not the kind of gross neglect that makes headlines, but it is relative neglect with a cumulative effect. Parents and caretakers are supposed to be mindful of proper nourishment. If they don't meet that role then the child can take on the job of making sure that he gets his snack. If the therapist simply provides the food, the child's lack of initiative and the parents' lack of caretaking doesn't get addressed.

The therapist plays a much more important role in bringing something like this to light, rather than taking on a function that's really not hers. So a therapist providing food can perpetuate a state of stuckness similar to that of a therapist providing physical affection. The child continues to not be in charge, in this case, of his hunger. He assumes a dependent position that the therapist would gratify and perpetuate if she provided food. Or which she would try to rectify if she addressed the fact that he was not acting as if he could take charge of his own needs.

Remember, our objective is to promote growth, and that needs to be reflected in how we think, what we say, and what we do about every matter that comes along, and of course it has to be reflected in our interventions.

QUESTION: And if we do that and our young patient now plans his snack with his mother and proudly brings it to his session, do we let him eat in our office?

ANSWER: What are you asking now?

QUESTION: When adult patients are in analysis we ask them not to smoke during their session because smoking distracts them or dulls their affective experience. For the same reason we don't want them drinking coffee during their analytic hour. I realize that smoking is no longer accepted in most offices for health reasons and eating or drinking on the couch is not really feasible. What I want to say is that with adults we would see eating and drinking during sessions as taking away from the intensity of the hour. Would this not be so with children as well?

ANSWER: Whether the patient is an adult or a child we still have to consider each of our interventions from a diagnostic point of view and from the perspective of where a patient is at this particular moment in treatment, and how what we do and say might affect him.

While food during sessions is something we might have questions about, there are adult patients who would be unable to tolerate being asked not to bring coffee to a session. They might need that cup of coffee as a distancing device, as a soother, or as a stimulant. They might not be able to analyze their need to drink coffee while in session with their therapist. They might not understand it from a symbolic perspective. Some adults are not able to think in symbols; their thinking is concrete. A patient like that might become confused or angry were we to question his need for coffee. Before raising a question like that, you might have to wait until the treatment reached a point where that patient could begin to analyze rather than act.

With a child, and particularly with a child who in the past came in a state of hunger and now takes pride in making sure that he has the snack he needs and who wants to show off his achievement, would we not very naturally accept his desire to share this with us and let him have his snack in our office? But what if his snack was something very gooey, something that could spill all over the furniture and make a mess? Would that be a hostile gesture? Would it be due to lack of awareness on his part? Or would it be something else altogether? Whatever was involved in the choice of food, if it endangered the intactness of our office, then we could talk about that, and maybe snacks could be chosen that don't make a mess. And after a while perhaps he would no longer have to show us what he was eating and simply eat it on the way to his appointment.

Whatever the issue, we need to know what we're doing and why. There are very few absolute rules that dictate our approach to treatment, but we do have to at least try to understand why we do what we do.

I remember Jenny, a perky 9-year-old girl who one day arrived for her session eating a large chocolate whipped-cream éclair. She sank into her chair, took a big bite, and with her mouth quite full said, "This is the best thing I've ever eaten in my whole life. All day I've been thinking about going to the Astor Bakery after school and getting one of these and bringing it here to show you. Would you like a bite? . . . it's so good, want to try some?"

It happens that this action on her part was very much tied to some work we had been doing for many months. The fact that she had been able to think about a treat for herself, plan and look forward to purchasing it, and then actually go and actualize her wish was a real triumph for her. By wanting me to be witness to this event I believe she was expressing her awareness that she had been able to carry out this action as a result of our work together. Even though it was, after all, just a cream puff, it represented a significant move on her part, a loosening of her unusually powerful defense of reaction formation. This young girl characteristically denied herself wanting, taking, having, and in general any use of her aggression in the service of pleasure and self-enhancement.

So you can see how we risk losing the point of a story again and again when we try to answer some of these seemingly *practical* questions out of context. These questions are never practical. They are always part of the total treatment situation. That doesn't mean we can't have some general restrictions on how the office is used. For instance, I'm not very happy about having messy food eaten in my office. Even though I was mindful of Jenny's achievement in being able to secure a treat for herself, I was uneasy about some of that whipped cream on my nice upholstered furniture. But it was possible to use the éclair incident therapeutically and still have some limits on food in the office. Most children can really manage to get their snack eaten on the way to their appointment and generally that's best, but sometimes we have to take our time in bringing this about.

QUESTION: How did you handle Jenny's éclair therapeutically and still eventually convey that such messy food was best kept out of the office?

ANSWER: When Jenny offered me a bite of her éclair she was just being polite. At least that's what she told me when I asked her what she would think if I really took a bite of her pastry. She said she offered without really thinking about it, just the way she would have done with her best friend or her brothers. She said she didn't always mean it when she made these offers. This éclair was really too good to give any of it away. She said that with her brothers it was dangerous to offer to share with them because they tended to eat the whole thing and leave nothing for her. On the other hand, if she didn't offer they just took it away. She said it was nice to offer some to a person like me because I knew how much she liked it and wouldn't take it away from her. She said she wanted to learn how to not give away what she had and how to not let her brothers bully her out of her things.

Jenny didn't bring any more éclairs to her sessions but "éclair" became a metaphor for finding within herself the ability to assume ownership of her desires in fantasy and in reality. You see, Jenny at 9 understood and was able to work within the therapeutic situation. That's not always the case, regardless of chronological age, and when it's not, we have to sometimes step in and make some rules.

QUESTION: What would you have done had Jenny dropped whipped cream all over your rug without the least bit of concern?

ANSWER: Probably something similar to what I did when an adult patient arrived on a very rainy day and tossed her dripping raincoat and umbrella on my couch. I asked her what was going on between us that she was making a mess on my couch. She tried to squiggle out of it by asking why I was making a big deal out of a random act on a wet and rainy night, but I persisted and we got quite a lot out of the incident.

I would try to approach a child in a similar way but there are times and there are children that require a simple but firm "I can't let you do that in my office," and when it happens again I might say, "I'm sure you remember that I don't allow that, so either you think you can change my mind or you think I didn't mean it. Or maybe it's something else. But whatever the reason, this is a rule that I cannot and will not let you break."

QUESTION: So sometimes it does come to that, to a flat rule imposed by the therapist and enforced without question.

ANSWER: Enforced, yes, but never without question. Questioning and being curious keeps our work alive and fresh.

So far we've discussed three kinds of situations that regularly come up in child treatment: that of a child wanting physical contact, the question of food during sessions, and the disengagement of the therapist's attention during a session. These situations also arise in adult treatment. Sometimes an adult will want to give us a hug because of some particular situation, such as leaving for a hospitalization, or losing a family member, or celebrating a longed-for pregnancy, and so forth. Similarly, adults sometimes bring food to sessions, and some adults create apathy or boredom in the therapist. Similar principles apply in our response to these situations.

Our goal is always to deepen the patient's treatment and further his development. What does it matter whether a patient wants to spill ink on our rug, bring a friend to his sessions, have us attend a school play or birthday party, or demand staying for two hours past the end of his appointment? These are all expressions of wishes. Our job is not to take them literally but to explore them. This applies equally whether the patient is a child or an adult.

QUESTION: I have a few more questions. I'm often confused when I have important information from the child's teacher or parent, and, although the child hasn't raised it, I feel I should mention it to the child. It always feels strange to bring in information I've gotten from another source.

ANSWER: How about an example?

QUESTION: Molly's mother told me that the family would be moving to a very far-away state in six months. The move is a big topic at home, yet Molly has never mentioned it to me. I feel we should be talking about this and about ending treatment, but I've been waiting for her to bring it up.

ANSWER: Why do you think she hasn't?

QUESTION: Maybe she doesn't want to face it; maybe it's denial. I know from her mother that she's very upset about leaving her friends, her school, and me.

ANSWER: It seems that the first order of business is to address her silence about something so important. I don't imagine that this is unusual for this child. Am I right?

QUESTION: Yes. She tends to keep upsetting things to herself and then nobody is there to help her and she has to struggle on her own. This has been a major theme in treatment. In fact, I thought we had made great progress in this area and now I see it's not so.

ANSWER: Don't assume that. Something as big as a move away from all that's familiar is enough to cause a regression in anyone. But it does look as if you need to follow the theme you've worked on regarding her silence about the move.

As for the general question regarding bringing in information gained from other sources, children know you talk to their parents and sometimes others, such as teachers and doctors. Still, there's no point in bringing it up unless you have a good reason to do so, for example, Molly's silence about the move. Just because you were handed information is not necessarily reason to bring it up. The only reason for bringing it up is if it has a therapeutic purpose.

QUESTION: What about getting on the floor with a child?

ANSWER: I don't know what you're asking.

QUESTION: Well, I'm not sure either. I think I'm asking something about the generation gap, about maintaining our adult stature and not becoming another child.

ANSWER: It's hard for me to imagine working with very young children and never getting down on the floor if they're playing on the floor with blocks or cars or some other toy that needs the expanse of the floor. But I think that's a matter of personal style. Surely sitting on the floor doesn't transform the therapist into a child, unless, of course, the therapist can't wait to send the car zooming across the room, or wants to build the tower taller.

I think you're asking an important question about how to join a child in play and yet maintain adult stature. The child needs you to remain the adult in charge, just as he needs his parents to be stronger, older, and wiser. But as you know, it isn't difficult for some adults to be playful and yet in control, while for others it's very difficult. So for a therapist to be able to tune in to play and yet be completely in command of the therapeutic environment can be very nourishing to certain children, nourishing in an ego-enhancing way.

Think for a minute about Kris's (1952) famous construct: "regression in the service of the ego." He talked about certain forms of regression that were necessary and growth promoting. The state of regression necessary for falling asleep and for being receptive to sexual pleasure are two examples of this. The ability to attune to and identify with infants and young children also stems from this form of regression. It allows the adult to enter the realm of play while retaining his caretaking capacities. This form of regression is very much a part of the therapist's experience with children and with adults. The capacity to play and to be playful are aspects of creativity (Sanville 1991, Winnicott 1971). They have an important place in our work with patients of all ages.

QUESTION: Would you ever choose an activity for a child?

ANSWER: I would like to say "never," but I can't. I've been with children who week after week just sat and neither talked, played, nor looked around. I found myself offering them various things on my shelves, and sometimes having a conversation with a puppet about the child in the room. I would ask the puppet whether he knew what Frankie liked to do and the puppet would say he didn't know and then I might mention what Frankie's parents told me about his love of cars and the puppet would say that couldn't be so since he never looked at my cars. I might go on that way for a while but even as I think about it now I don't like it very much because it sounds too light, too much like entertainment.

So, to better answer your question, there are extreme situations in which you might pick an activity for a child out of desperation, but as a general rule, it's not the way we usually work. It's a little like picking the subject of a session with an adult patient. We don't do that except under very extreme circumstances. I've worked with several very withdrawn adults who found it almost impossible to initiate any dialogue with me. Some of them requested that I get them started by asking some questions. I tried to find a way of making the questions different from social exchanges. My goal was to help these patients no longer need my help in talking. I think choosing an activity for a child has an analogous basis.

QUESTION: What about a child cheating during checkers or board games? What's a good way to think about that in a therapy session?

ANSWER: I like the way you phrased that, since it already contains the idea that cheating has a different meaning in the therapy situation, or at least that it's up to the therapist to give it a different meaning. When a child cheats I say something like this: "When you come here and we play games, you can change the rules any way you want. That's one of the differences between the kind of playing we do and playing with your friends, brothers, parents, and everyone else. But the difference between here and outside is that outside if you change the rules people will be mad at you. I will not be mad at you when you change the rules but we will talk about why you change them."

Then, whenever I notice the child has "changed" the rules I will mention it and ask whether the new rules apply to me as well as to him. At some point I try to take this a bit further and explore the issue of winning and losing and what he's trying to achieve. I've found this approach pretty productive.

QUESTION: I have a question that's on a completely different subject but it popped into my head because the topic of cheating reminded me of some of my conversations with teachers and their very different attitudes about such matters as cheating. Of course they have to uphold rules, their situation is very different from ours, but still, sometimes they do get very judgmental about the children they teach. One such teacher was very insistent that I visit his class and observe my patient in that situation. My patient, Allen, age 7, was causing a lot of trouble in the class, in contrast to being very pleasant and engaging during his sessions with me. The teacher and I both felt we had very different perceptions of this child. The teacher wanted me to see Allen *in action* at school. I was very torn about making such a visit. Do you have a point of view on this?

ANSWER: I do, but as you can probably predict by now, it's not a simple "yes, go" or "no, don't go" approach. In the situation you describe, and as you describe it, it sounds as if your reason for going would be to satisfy the teacher's request, and that's not usually a good enough reason. It also sounds as if the teacher is telling you that you don't know how difficult this child is for him, for the teacher. That's important but not necessarily a good reason for making a school visit. Possibly the teacher wants to be able to talk to you about this child, or perhaps about himself. You can find out quite a bit about this on the telephone.

There are occasions when a school visit might be called for, but there should be a very strong reason for such a departure from our usual role with our patients. Sometimes a school is ready to ask a child to leave and transfer to another school. Generally that's something the parents would handle, but in some situations, if such a move would be very detrimental to the child at this time, the presence of the child's therapist could help to quiet a potentially explosive situation. If the child is very disruptive or very withdrawn, the therapist or the school might be able to arrange for a student teacher or talented paraprofessional to be in the class-room and help that child. Were this kind of school visit to take place, there would be no need for the therapist to visit the child's class unless descriptions of his behavior in the classroom differed so much from his behavior at home or in therapy sessions that the therapist might want to see what was actually going on in the classroom. Of course there are extraordinary situations that might create a need to depart from our usual work with patients of any age. But unless there is a very good reason for such a departure, we're best off maintaining our usual role, which is to see our patients in our offices and occasionally speak to them on the telephone if that's called for.

10

❧

What Do We Do with Dangerous Secrets, Personal Questions, Gifts, Therapy Sessions Outside the Office . . . ?

QUESTION: What if a child wants you to keep a secret and the secret has serious implications?

ANSWER: I need an example.

QUESTION: Miles, age 10, told me he'd been having such bad headaches that twice now he thinks he blacked out. He doesn't want his parents to know because they'd get upset and start yelling at him or at each other.

ANSWER: What did you do?

QUESTION: I told him bad headaches like that were too important to ignore. They needed the attention of a doctor. I asked him why he was so sure his parents would fight and yell rather than help. He didn't know, but he just couldn't tell them. I asked if he would be okay with my telling them. At first he was reluctant. I told him there were many ways of tackling such a big problem and we would work hard to find one that felt okay to him but we couldn't ignore something as important as these painful headaches.

I told him one possibility was that I meet with his parents with him present; then they would not be as likely to yell at him or even at each other. He didn't like that. I said I could tell them over the phone. He didn't like that. I said I could tell them during one of my regular appointments with either one or both of his parents. He wasn't sure; he didn't think so.

I told him that now I was having a problem and we had to find a solution. On the one hand I didn't want to do anything that would break my rule of keeping what we talk about private. We need that rule very much. How could he trust me if I broke a rule so important and essential to our work? On the other hand how could I be a trustworthy person if I allowed his headaches to continue without medical attention? I told him he was giving me a tough situation to handle, and did he understand my dilemma?

As I said all this I remember feeling very distressed and frustrated. Perhaps he heard that in my tone and manner, for at that point he agreed to let me tell his mom in person. I was lucky. What if he hadn't?

ANSWER: Perhaps if you had not allowed your genuine concern to come through, if you had remained coolly neutral, he would have still refused to let you tell. Perhaps the affective component in your expressing the dilemma you were faced with tipped the scales. Perhaps he recognized the depth of your concern, felt the caring about him that it represented, and so could in turn empathize with the position you were in. If that's what happened, what a nice example of a dilemma turning into a growth-producing event!

But you're wise to wonder about a different outcome, one in which you've been entrusted with a serious secret but sworn to secrecy. When that happens we sometimes have to risk losing the patient by placing life and death matters and serious health and safety considerations first.

I'll give you an example from my own practice. Once, during a first session with an adolescent boy, he told me that he had attempted suicide twice and described the attempts in detail. After each of these attempts, his best friend's brother, who is a medical intern, took care of him. After the first attempt this young intern agreed not to tell anyone, but after the second he insisted that the patient tell his parents and seek the help of a therapist. My patient never told his parents about the suicide attempts but he did make up a reason for seeing a therapist that was acceptable to them. He told them he had doubts about going to college and needed to work this conflict out with someone outside the family. He knew his parents would do anything to get him to go to college.

During our consultation, this 16-year-old boy told me he was probably going to attempt suicide again. I told him I was going to have to tell his parents, realizing, of course, that I was betraying a trust. I was making this decision because his life was my number one priority. I told him that because of my intended breach of confidentiality, we would not be able to work together. I was sorry about that but I would find him a very fine therapist. I told him I was sorry we would not be working together and wished him the best. I told his parents about the suicide attempts. I will never forget his mother's response, for it shocked me more than any statement I've ever heard in all my years of practice. She said, "Do you realize you are violating patient–doctor confidentiality? Isn't this a breach of ethics on your part?" This was said in a cold, harsh tone. I told her that indeed I did realize I was violating confidentiality and that I was doing it with her son's knowledge. As far as my ethics were concerned, I felt that the boy's life was my prime concern. I then explained that my action had disqualified me from treating their son and that I therefore proposed they consult a colleague whom I held in high esteem. They did, and I learned the young man did quite well, went to college, and made no further suicide attempts.

Of course, it's most likely that in telling his parents I was doing exactly what he wished me to do, that he very much wanted his parents to know he had tried to kill himself, but would never have admitted this wish.

Now you might wonder why I was so quick to refer him to another therapist and not try to get his permission to tell his parents, or, failing that, try to work out my breach of confidentiality. At the time of this consultation I did not feel up to working with a suicidal adolescent. My practice was very demanding at the time and I was feeling somewhat burned out. It seemed a bad time to take on such a big responsibility. Under that circumstance I felt my decision was better for him and better for me.

QUESTION: Our work gets very difficult sometimes, and then on top of that we get faced with these life and death issues. It's helpful to think of placing these monumental issues ahead of confidentiality, and it's helpful to place value on our peace of mind.

ANSWER: There are also legal and ethical issues to consider in such situations. We have an obligation to report such serious matters to the parents. We really have no right not to, not from an ethical, legal, or human point of view, and if we neglect this responsibility the consequences could be tragic and could also lead to a lawsuit. We have to protect our patient *and* ourselves.

QUESTION: On a much lighter note, there's a tricky issue that comes up a lot. It has to do with answering personal questions. Sometimes children ask me whether I have children, how old I am, whether I live in my office, whether I have a husband, a daddy, a mommy, what kind of a car I drive, whether I've seen a particular movie, and many more questions that all have to do with me and my life. I try not to answer them. I try to make therapeutic use of them by exploring them, by asking the child what he thinks, how he would like me to answer his question. Sometimes I find a way of using these questions to further the child's treatment. Every once in a while, though, I get into an impasse with a child who insists on getting a real answer and becomes very upset and angry when the answer is not forthcoming. What do you suggest? Should I just answer the question? Sometimes this issue grows so big, the child becomes so distraught, that I fear the working alliance will go down the drain and the case will end if I don't comply.

ANSWER: You sound pretty clear about not wanting to answer personal questions. You also sound as if you have a pretty good approach to not answering them, but instead turning them into something useful and trying to make them work therapeutically. So the main problem you have is with an occasional child who won't take "no" for an answer. Is that right?

QUESTION: Yes. With most children it doesn't become a major issue. The most common question I get is whether I have children. Girls ask that; I can't recall any boy asking it. Boys are more likely to ask me whether I play a sport they like or what kind of car I have. Personal questions from boys are very rare. Even though I can usually handle these questions without answering them, I dread being asked. So it's really not true that I only have trouble with the occasional child who insists on an answer. I find the whole area of personal questions troubling. I like my personal life to stay separate.

ANSWER: Besides your preference for privacy, how do you understand your patients' curiosity about your personal life?

QUESTION: Well, it's not any one thing. One little girl will ask me whether I have kids because she's feeling very close to me and really wants to *be* one of my kids at that moment. Another child will ask me whether I have kids for fear that she has some powerful rivals for my affection. A teen, a high-school junior who is visiting colleges, will ask me what college I attended, a simple-sounding question, yet loaded with meaning on multiple levels. The variations are endless . . . I hate these questions.

ANSWER: Do you understand what you dislike so much about being asked these questions?

QUESTION: Well, doesn't every therapist?

ANSWER: No. I do agree that sometimes a patient's insistence that we answer a personal question, and their anger if we don't, becomes difficult to deal with and draining as well. This is so both with adults and children. But you see, we know that by answering their question we would simply cause our patients to exchange one set of frustrations for another. We would gratify their wish to know, which they think would be helpful to them, but in so doing we might also convey the impression that they had overpowered us. For some patients, that feeling of superior power might feel good, or good and bad in some combination, but that would be temporary. Ultimately it would most likely feel more bad than good because patients need us to be strong and well grounded.

QUESTION: But don't they also need us to be flexible and not so wedded to our professional stance that we can't be understanding of their request even if it steps a little outside of what's customary?

ANSWER: Well, the real question is what you mean by being "understanding" of their request. I'll give you an example of one of those *simple* requests that grew to dominate a treatment situation. Although it concerns the treatment of an adult, as you'll see, it's relevant to the treatment of children.

For many years I treated a woman who divorced her husband after starting treatment with me. Her decision to divorce predated our working together, but she waited to initiate the divorce proceedings until we had worked together for a year. Now you might think that during that year of therapy she had gained insight into her wish to divorce and was able to proceed for that reason. I wish that were true, but it's not the case. Her being able to proceed with the divorce had more to do with having formed a connection with me, a factor that made it seem less frightening to her to leave her husband. She was an isolated person, friendships were difficult for her, and after a while her treatment became the center of her life.

Although she had been eager to leave her husband and the atmosphere of unpleasantness that had grown between them, and despite her relief at coming home each night to a peaceful, quiet apartment, she nonetheless eventually became lonely. She wondered whether she would ever find another mate, one who was kinder and less critical of her. One day she asked me whether I had ever been divorced. She had noted my wedding band but wondered whether it might be from a remarriage rather than a first marriage. She said if she knew I had been able to leave a bad marriage for a good one it would give her hope that this was possible for her too.

For the next few years this patient often repeated her request that I tell her about myself. Much as I tried to explore it, my patient was not interested. She just wanted to know the answer. She did not want to understand the question.

While this was a woman of high intelligence, she lacked symbolic capacities. Her cognitive development had outpaced her emotional growth. Consider what it might mean for an adult woman to really believe that if a person she values can remarry, so can she. Think of the information contained in such a belief. It speaks to a level of object relations we would be more likely to see in a very young child. And there was good reason for this arrest, for this woman had suffered major traumas during childhood. The particular traumas had left her with a lifelong struggle with issues of identity, autonomy, and object connection. Her question about the history of my marriage was the concretization of her desire to be able to feel hope, hope that loss could be replaced by something good, by gain, by connection, by love.

QUESTION: And what did you do with her question?

ANSWER: I did all the usual things. I tried to understand it, to explore it, and so forth. But one day when she was particularly adamant about getting an answer and her tone reflected urgency and desperation, I finally realized that on some level, she believed that her whole future rested on my answer. With this insight I responded to her much as I had to the little boy who told me he would *die* if I didn't allow him to take home an office truck. Remember, I had said the following to the little boy:

"Wouldn't it be terrible if I really believed that you would *die* if you didn't have this truck!? I wouldn't be much help to you if I believed a thing like that! Why the next thing might be that you'd believe it too!" (Chapter 6, p. 87).

What I finally said to this adult woman was along the same lines. I told her that she had created a fantastic equation in which her fate is inextricably linked to mine. I would be joining her in this fantasy if I satisfied her question with an answer. What we needed to do together was to understand her difficulty in having wishes for herself, for having aspirations for her future, for being able to feel hopeful that they could be realized. Her interest in my history was very useful but only if we viewed it as a metaphor, the leitmotif of her life in which loss was replaced by more loss and now she is wondering whether there can be a different sequel to loss, loss followed by renewal and redemption.

QUESTION: And were you able to interest her in this approach? Did she give up wanting an answer?

ANSWER: Not entirely, but I did pique her curiosity enough to allow us to explore the effect of her early losses on her lack of expectation that good things could happen to her. And that did lead to insight into her attempt to fill this void, this desolate anticipation of an empty future, by linking up with me, by wanting to know her future by knowing my present. You see, there was a very positive aspect to her asking me about my life, however concretized, however fantastic. It was an object connection and it represented hope.

QUESTION: I've noticed you put a lot of stock in hope. Why is that?

ANSWER: *With our adult patients, it's often hope that brings them into our consulting rooms; it's often hope that holds out the possibility that there's a way to change and grow and have a better life. I know it appears that it's pain and dissatisfaction that bring people to a therapist's office, but if you think about it, isn't it really the hope beneath that makes them pick up the phone and make that initial call? Hope is the basis for the working alliance. It's the prime motive to persist in the treatment situation.*

Now with children it's a little different. They are brought to see us. It's not their decision to come. But when things go right, the therapy situation becomes a place of hope for them too. When I say things go right, all I mean is there's a dawning awareness that this new stranger really wants to understand them.

QUESTION: Have you ever answered a personal question?

ANSWER: I have. I'm not saying I'm correct in doing so, but the one question that I have on occasion answered when asked by parents is about my having children. Some parents, when consulting me about their child at an initial meeting, have told me that it was very important for them to know whether I, too, have children. The implication was that I couldn't possibly understand them if I didn't have children of my own. In some of these cases I've answered them. But I can't really explain this response of mine in a satisfactory manner. I know full well that some of our most gifted child therapists have not had children. Anna Freud comes to mind as a prime example. We also know that some of the most talented teachers are childless. Clearly being a parent has little to do with understanding children or their parents. So my behavior makes no sense on a conscious level.

On the most obvious level, when a parent asks this question, I'm being asked whether I will understand what they're going through as parents. The question suggests that a particular value is being placed on my being a fellow parent, that it's being viewed as a form of assurance that my understanding of them will be forthcoming. But why? After all, we all encounter many situations in our work with patients that we have no personal experience with. There are the extraordinary life events like those of Holocaust survivors and others who have lost everyone and everything and had to flee for their life to escape a totalitarian government or a natural disaster. We are not asked to share in their background. We encounter patients who have learned they have a fatal, degenerative illness, and it's assumed that we'll be able to help them live out what time remains and prepare them for death. We meet parents who have learned their child is autistic, or retarded, or has a chronic physical condition that will prevent him or them from ever again having the privilege of living an ordinary life. We attend to all these extreme situations despite having had no similar experience in our own lives.

Then there are the more common but no less wrenching heartbreaks such as infertility, divorce, death of a spouse, and so forth. We don't feel we have to have lived through these painful life events to understand those of our patients who have. What we do need is to *listen* and allow our patients to teach us what we need to know.

This is a very long detour into saying that sometimes personal information is requested by a patient because the patient wants the assurance that we've had an experience similar to theirs, a common ground, so to speak, that will guarantee our understanding of what they're going through. Well, much as the patient might believe this, is it really so, and is it really so simple? Of course not.

And this is not the only reason we are given when personal information is asked for. Sometimes it has to do with our credentials. The patient or parent wants to know where we went to college and graduate school, and something about our training as psychotherapists, our orientation, how long we've been in practice, what type of patient population we specialize in, how many children we've treated, and how long the average treatment lasts. Some of these questions are answerable and relevant and some are not. Most important is that in most cases, the answers we might provide do not address the real question being asked.

QUESTION: What *is* the real question being asked?

ANSWER: If it's a parent of a child for whom treatment has been recommended, the parent might be asking whether the therapist is well trained, competent, and trustworthy. Now everyone would agree that that's a responsible attitude for any parent to take. However, most of the answers to these questions do little to provide the sought-for information. What would be of much greater use is the attitude of the therapist when asked these questions and the spirit in which they're addressed.

QUESTION: Would you give me an example of how you might respond to a string of questions about your training?

ANSWER: It would depend completely on who asked and the tone in which it was asked. Is it being asked by a person who might know the difference between a Freudian orientation and a self psychological one? Is it being asked with sincerity or is it being asked in an imperious tone?

You would need to hone in on your general impression of the person asking the question. Being asked personal questions about our lives, or what appears on the surface as less personal because it's related to our training, requires us to respond with the same care as with any other communication between patient and therapist.

When a parent asks me about my training during the consultation phase, I am willing to answer some questions, but only up to a point. Then I might tell a parent that choosing a therapist for her child is a pretty awesome undertaking. I understand how hard it is to judge the person's talent and competence. However, there are ways of accomplishing this. Of course it's important to make sure the therapist has the proper training and license to practice. That's the easy part. But assessing the more subtle qualities in a therapist, qualities that play such an important part in the treatment process, that's the more difficult part. I suggest that the parent not rush a decision, but spend as much time with me as necessary to gain an impression of how helpful and competent I am at my work. This will be revealed by the way I listen, ask questions, remember what I've been told, and convey a growing understanding of the situation they've set before me. I urge them not to place their child under my care until they've spent sufficient time with me to feel that they're comfortable with such a decision. If, after several meetings with me, they do not feel confidence in my ability to be helpful, I urge them to meet another therapist. The point is that the parent can get to have a pretty good sense of what I'm like by talking about themselves, their child, and the reasons that brought them to my office. They do not need me to answer personal questions to gain insight into what I'm like and how I work.

When children ask questions we have somewhat different considerations to keep in mind. After all, their questions are not designed to help them decide whether the therapist is the right person for them. What we have to consider when faced with personal questions from children is why they might be asking them and whether they would be able to tolerate the frustration of not getting an answer. A child's ability to tolerate not getting an answer to his question, but rather allowing it to be turned into an exploration of his curiosity, could indicate ego strength and the beginning of a working alliance, or it could indicate a type of passivity at being thwarted. In the case of passivity, the exploration would not go far since it might be prompted by compliance rather than by curiosity.

If a child's frustration at not being given an answer is very intense, we have to consider various possibilities at our end that would prevent the child from feeling injured and rejected by our refusal. With some children, from the beginning of treatment I've introduced the idea that some things in therapy are different from any other place in the world. I've presented my not answering questions, but welcoming them for discussion purposes, as one of those features special to the therapy work. With some children I've even gone so far as to say it's against the therapy rules, just as is hanging up their pictures or letting them take home therapy toys. But this last "rule" must be presented with care, for there might be questions you would want to answer. One such question might be where you will be during vacation, in case you want to make it possible for your young patient to write to you.

The same care that goes into considering children's questions should go into considering those of their parents. Our response here, as in all matters, should be based on our understanding of the patients before us. I admitted earlier having at times answered a question so often asked by parents regarding my having children. I realize that answering this is an idiosyncrasy of mine. Or so it seems since I cannot think of a good reason why I make this exception.

QUESTION: We've covered a lot of ground today. I have one more question, but it seems pretty slight, after what we just talked about. It has to do with giving gifts to a child patient on special occasions such as birthdays or termination.

ANSWER: There is nothing slight about the subject of gifts. Nothing is really slight in the treatment process. All these matters are important and should be treated with respect. Every communication represents a conscious and unconscious cluster of wishes and desires, fears and anxieties, and often conflict as well. Understanding these communications demands putting to use our greatest sensitivity and combining it with a line of thinking and theory building already spanning close to a century and continuing to evolve.

There is nothing simple about wanting to give or receive a gift. A gift, whether offered by the patient or requested of the therapist, can be understood on every psychosexual level. I repeat that within the psychotherapy situation all the normal social exchanges assume new dimensions.

As usual it helps to enrich these discussions when we have a clinical example to work with. Do you have a particular clinical example of a dilemma around gift giving?

QUESTION: Yes. Young children and children of latency age often want a gift from me for special occasions such as Christmas, Hanukkah, their birthdays, graduation, even Valentine's Day. I have a very hard time knowing how to handle these requests.

ANSWER: How do these requests come up?

QUESTION: Sometimes a child will tell me about his birthday coming up and the party that's being planned, will mention what his parents are going to give him and then ask me whether I'm going to give him a gift as well. At that point I'm already feeling uncomfortable because if I explore his question, this exploration might seem a hypothetical discussion to me, but to the child it might seem as if we're planning his gift. So I feel stuck because I don't want to mislead him.

ANSWER: A simple approach would be to say to him something like this: "You know what a special place this is, and that here we think about everything we do so carefully. So knowing that, what do you think is going to happen here with me about giving you a gift?"

QUESTION: And if the child gets upset and says he just wants a "yes" or a "no," he doesn't want to discuss and understand it . . . why can't I just give him a present for his birthday like everyone else?

ANSWER: Then you could say that now it sounds as if he would like a present from you. You're not saying what you're going to do about that but you would like to know what he had in mind.

QUESTION: Suppose he says he wants a particular video game that several of his friends have, and his parents won't get it for him because it's too expensive and too violent.

Actually this exact situation came up with an 8-year-old boy. I felt very awkward about the whole thing. I'm not crazy about video games; I think they're overused. Most of them are mindless, and they're often violent. I can't think of a gift I would enjoy giving less. Then there's the issue of its being expensive. It's not appropriate for me to give expensive gifts to my patients, nor do I want to incur that kind of expense. Then there's the fact that his parents don't want him to have it, so how can I go against their wishes and be willing to spend more money on their son than they are?

ANSWER: What a great example! This child wants you to give him a toy that breaks every rule. It's expensive, violent, forbidden by his parents, and possibly has nothing to do with what you've been working on in therapy.

QUESTION: Now that you mention it, it does have something to do with a major theme in his treatment. He thinks he looks like a sissy, goody-goody kind of kid. His teachers like him, his parents' friends like him, he gets good grades, and the tough boys don't include him in their play.

ANSWER: Well, that's fascinating. It sounds to me as if his request gives you a lot to work with. What's holding you back?

QUESTION: I failed to see it. I got preoccupied by the request and failed to see the big picture. Maybe I have trouble with his wanting to become a tough guy. He's such pleasure to be with just the way he is. This discussion is taking a very unexpected turn. We began by talking about gift giving and I ran into a countertransferential problem that really obstructed my understanding of what was happening with my patient. Now that I've been

alerted to this situation it no longer seems very complicated. I can interpret the wish represented by the gift he
requested. I can tell him that working on the wish to be
tougher and stronger will do much more for him than a
video game.

But could you give me some guidelines about gifts in
general? Isn't it sometimes appropriate to give a child a
gift?

ANSWER: You won't find great agreement among therapists
about this matter. Some give gifts liberally, others never. As
in all these matters, I like to look at the total diagnostic picture, assess the child's ability to deal with gratification and
frustration, and deal with each incident as it comes up. And
I do have some guidelines.

If I deemed it appropriate to give a child a gift, I would
want it to be related to the work we've done together. I would
want it to be something durable rather than something
flimsy. I would want it to be planned with the child ahead
of time, rather than a surprise. I would not want it to be
expensive, and I would want to be sure the parents knew
about it in advance, so that they were not surprised by it
either.

I'll give you some examples of presents I've given either
for a birthday, or at termination, or even before a long summer break.

I had a young patient who from his first day in my office
particularly loved a very small, well-made toy motorcycle on
my office toys shelf. He told me he liked it better than all
my cars because it came with a rider and my cars were all
empty of people. During the course of treatment it became
clear to him and to me that the motorcycle and rider represented him at his best: strong, skillful, and special. Many a
time he begged me to let him take the motorcycle and rider
home "just for the weekend." I didn't allow it. But as we
approached termination he wondered whether I would get

him a duplicate of the motorcycle as a therapy "souvenir." I did.

Another example of a gift I considered to have value for a particular child was a clock with an alarm. Cara was precociously responsible in the way children sometimes become when they have parents who are overly casual about time, food, sleep, and clothing, and really all aspects of child care. Cara couldn't bear that she was late to school almost every day. During the course of our work we had talked about her growing ability to take care of certain things on her own. She could make her own breakfast, pick out her clothes, dress appropriately for the weather that day, and have all her school books and whatever else she needed packed in her backpack. Her big worry was waking up in time. Her parents often were very late in waking her and so she tried to wake herself but would end up sleeping poorly. After much discussion we decided that I would give her her own alarm clock as a present for her eighth birthday.

She could have asked her parents for a clock but they already teased her about being "uptight," not like them. A clock would have brought on more teasing. My giving it to her deflected some of the attention from her onto me. They saw me as very precise with my neat office and my predictable schedule. They told me they liked me despite my being "uptight."

Cara loved having her own clock and was able to sleep more peacefully with the knowledge that the alarm would go off at the time she wanted. But in addition to her improved sleep and peace of mind was another important factor about the clock. It represented her therapist's affirmation that her standards for order and organization were not an "uncool" defect but a valuable aspect of her character, her personality, and her striving for independence.

QUESTION: I understand these examples, but have you ever refused to give a child gifts no matter how often you were asked?

ANSWER: Yes, I remember a particular example of my not giving gifts despite being asked over and over again. This took place in an agency and concerned a 10-year-old boy whose therapist had left and I was hired to fill the vacancy. This child was then transferred to me. In reading his admirably detailed case record, thick with process narratives of sessions spanning two years, I noted that most of their verbal exchanges centered around his asking for toy cars and the therapist complying with his requests. The child was one of those brilliant psychotic children who develop a particular expertise that they adhere to with great exclusivity. Cars were his life, or so it seemed. His previous therapist certainly behaved as if cars kept him from falling apart, and the young patient did anything he could to confirm that image. Many of their sessions were spent going out to look at cars or to buy miniature ones for his collection.

I was a beginning therapist at the time and I read with great interest this record of three-times-a-week treatment for two years in which nothing ever changed. But my interest was tinged with dismay at the absolute narrowness of the focus of the treatment and at the therapist's complete acceptance of the perseverative nature of the sessions.

When I first met Matt he immediately began his car talk by listing cars by make, year, style, and description of special features. This was all said in a monotonous tone of voice with a great deal of rocking. I didn't quite know what to do with myself or how to fit myself in. After about twenty minutes of car monologue, during which I wasn't sure that he was aware of my presence, he switched gears and began directing his talking towards me. I'm choosing my words with care for he was not talking *to* me but rather directing his words in my direction. The content of his words went like this: "So will you get me the red matchbox convertible #2234 or will you get me the yellow miniature fire engine #7642, and can we go to the store now and look at them and maybe we'll see a 1976 Jaguar on the street, and in the store maybe they will have a double decker red bus . . . and will you buy me that as well?"

I remember shocking myself and Matt by saying a firm "No, we can't do that. That's not what you and I are going to do." I then went on to explain that he can go look at cars with any number of other people, and that other people can buy him cars for his collection. But what I can do with him is something only a therapist can do. I can listen to him, understand him, and work to make him feel comfortable. He then actually looked at me and stopped rocking.

Over the next two years he would periodically lapse into the old perseverative car talk, and with it came a string of requests, but when that happened I would know he was upset about something and that this was his way of expressing it. So I would say to him, "When you talk car talk that way it usually means that something has upset you. Do you know what it was?" He often didn't know what had upset him but together we would try to uncover it, and a lot of good work went on.

By having read that long record describing Matt's prior treatment, which focused heavily on gift giving, I had learned an important lesson. The presents had been detrimental to Matt's growth. What they had done was infantilize him, and this had interfered with the development of his inner resources and general growth.

QUESTION: You said in passing that Matt's former therapist had gone outside with him. When is that appropriate? I tend to think therapy should take place in the office.

ANSWER: I agree with you, but many therapists will go for a walk with a patient, play catch in the park, go have an ice cream and such. I personally don't agree with this approach, although I've been told by some of my colleagues that some children and adolescents feel too confined by the therapy office to stay there for forty-five minutes. I sometimes wonder who feels too confined, the patient or the therapist?

By leaving the office, the therapist and patient relinquish some of the uniqueness of the therapeutic environment, a setting in which two people, in a familiar space with no distraction from the world outside, both strive for a common goal, the growth of the patient.

One fortuitous by-product of the growth of the patient is that it so often spurs the growth of the therapist. My work with Matt gave me such an opportunity. Here I was, a beginner, taking over the case of a more practiced therapist, and rather than following her lead I went in a very different direction. I made demands on this child who previously had only been gratified. I expected more of him, I saw more in him, and he was able to rise to my expectations and reach a higher and more satisfying level of functioning and feeling. It was a very exciting experience to witness his growth and to share in the pleasure and hope his parents felt at the changes in him.

I think we've often witnessed parents who give gifts of candy and toys not because they choose to, or want to, but because they don't want the fuss that might follow were they to refuse to grant their child's request. Such occasional gift giving by default is pretty understandable under the rushed and often pressured circumstances of most people's lives. But when gifts become a kind of ransom extracted by children from their parents, and the parents helplessly pay it, then we have a situation that erodes something precious in the parent–child relationship. It's very important for therapists to note the appearance of this dynamic in the treatment process and interpret it, rather than yielding to the demand.

CHAPTER
11

Child Treatment When
Parents Divorce

QUESTION: Sometimes parents consult us when they're
    about to separate, or perhaps they've already begun di-
    vorce proceedings. They request our help in finding ways
    of sparing their child the pain of divorce. I'm now talk-
    ing about situations where the request for help is not in
    response to any manifestations of disturbance of mood
    or behavior in their child. The request is perceived by the
    parents as a preventative measure. How do we handle
    such requests?

ANSWER: Perhaps the enormity of your question reflects some-
    thing about the way you feel when parents approach you with
    such a request.

QUESTION: I think that's so. In some of these situations I've
    felt as if I was being handed the entire responsibility for
    how the child would survive the divorce.

ANSWER: Did you try to analyze why your reaction was so extreme?

QUESTION: I did, but it didn't help much. I've been through a divorce myself and I have children who were deeply affected by the experience, so of course that has something to do with the strength of my reaction. But still, when I try to analyze something that's getting in my way I usually succeed to some extent. In this area I have very little insight.

ANSWER: Well, it's not my place to analyze you but rather to deal with your question in a more supervisory and educational manner. Perhaps discussing the subject will lift some of your intense reaction and will lead to a way of thinking about this that's helpful.

Parental divorce and its aftermath usually presents us with very difficult, very challenging situations. In order to do good work we have to be really clear about our role. What is our function with the child and with his parents? Does our role change in any way when the parents are divorcing? What do you think?

QUESTION: Well, actually it shouldn't change. We are still primarily there as the child's therapist but we are also there to help the parents. Our role with the parents is less defined than our role with the child. I guess that's the root of the problem. Our role with the parents is often unclear even under the so-called "normal" circumstances of an intact family. It grows even more muddy during the very tumultuous atmosphere created by divorce.

ANSWER: So what you're saying is that our lack of clarity about our role with parents is augmented by the stress and disruptions experienced by divorcing parents, by their increased demands on us, and possibly by what we see happening to the child as a result of all this strain and uncertainty. If we could feel clearer about our role with parents, wouldn't we be on firmer ground, more able to stay centered and focused whatever the circumstances?

QUESTION: That sounds very good but how do you do that when you have a hysterical mother calling and begging you to do something fast to prevent her husband's effort to get custody of their child? Or when that irate father calls to say that his son's appointment hour cuts into his visiting time with his son, and upon hearing that you can't change his son's time, threatens to pull him out of treatment? On top of that there's the mother's lawyer calling to say they need an affidavit to the effect that the child should not sleep at his father's house on school nights, and then you have the father's lawyer asking you to come to *his* office to discuss your impressions of the child and the child's relationships with each of his parents.

ANSWER: Being well grounded and clear about our role and function as a child therapist is basic and essential to your work at all times, but under the particularly taxing circumstances imposed by parents who are in the process of divorcing, the very *survival* of our effectiveness depends on it. Just think: the parents are divorcing, the child's life is about to be altered forever, but you, the therapist, must stay the same. Your ability to stay the same is going to be of enormous help to the child and ultimately to the parents, although they might not see it that way when you start turning down their requests.

Take, for instance, the father who angrily demands that you change his child's therapy appointment and threatens to pull him out of treatment if you don't comply. How do you understand his behavior? What is your diagnostic impression of him?

QUESTION: This man was none too pleased to have his child in treatment with me from the outset. He wanted his son, who, by the way, is 6 years old, to go to someone who had been highly recommended by his therapist. When they met this "highly recommended" person they learned that he charged a very high fee. Also, the mother found him very cold, so between the high fee and the cold manner I was picked as being the lesser evil.

ANSWER: Although you meant "lesser evil" as a joke, let's think a minute why you made that particular joke. You were more affordable and not as cold, but where does "evil" come in?

QUESTION: I was recommended by Mrs. B., the mother's therapist. The father feels that Mrs. B. is responsible for the dissolution of his marriage. Of course his reaction is not uncommon. We know how frequently one partner of a couple feels that the therapist of his spouse is causing trouble. Well, in this case the father was convinced that his wife's therapist was an irresponsible, card-carrying, ardent feminist who had destroyed his marriage, and some of his anger at her was displaced onto me. Before the divorce process started, his anger at me was sporadic and manageable. The pattern was that he would get upset about something he thought I was mishandling in his son's treatment and would come in and discuss it with me. For instance, upon learning from his son that we had played cards during the session he would get agitated. He felt that playing cards wasn't real "therapy." It seemed to him a waste of time, a sham. Why wasn't I doing what I was hired for, instead of doing what any friend or baby-sitter could do? He would tell me this and we would talk about it. These discussions were usually helpful and productive, and he would leave my office feeling much better and quite satisfied to have his son in treatment with me. But the good feeling wouldn't last, and we would soon have to meet again to restore his confidence in me.

I realize, as I talk about him, that his representation of me as a "good" object could never survive for long. His aggressive-destructive wishes would take over and the "good" object representations would begin to fade. He was not unaware of this pattern in himself but he had little ability to modulate his affects, his moods, and his attacks of anger and suspicion. So you're right to have picked up on my use of the word "evil" in this context. "Evil" is what he transformed me into over and over again. Then, we would meet face to face, and the good representation of me would be restored. However, once his wife initiated the divorce, my "evil" status no longer had that fluctuating pattern. It became permanent. I became a displacement of his wife, her therapist, and ultimately the "bad" punishing mother of his childhood. When that happened, I found I could no longer connect with him.

Look, I understand this father and his dynamics, but what do I do with all this insight?

ANSWER: You wouldn't ask that question if you were treating an adult who manifested this pattern. If this man were your actual patient, you would, at the proper time, make an interpretation and follow it up with many more as you continued to work on this central issue in the patient's life. But in the case you described you're treating a child and this man is the child's father. Even though this man is not, in the formal sense, your patient, you know some basic things about him, but you're suddenly unable to put them to good use. Yet prior to the divorce proceedings you had developed a modus operandi for restoring and maintaining your working alliance with him, shaky though it was. So perhaps you have to ask yourself this: What happened to you that you've become helpless in this situation? What happened that all you've learned about this man is no longer informing your approach to him, your ability to connect with him, or sustaining your empathy for him?

QUESTION: You're right. I've let myself off the hook too much, making excuses about how this situation is too complicated and not at all what my work is about. I've justified my not taking hold of the total picture by saying to myself that I'm here to work with 6-year-old Andy, who's a pretty scared little boy. I've stuck to the position that I'm here to help Andy feel more safe. I've rationalized that I'm not here to deal with an angry father, a hysterical mother, and combative lawyers. Andy needs my help and I'm equipped to provide it, but I'm not equipped to deal with all the chaos that's been generated by this divorce, nor do I want any part of it. To answer your question, I'm too angry and overwhelmed by what's happening to be able to use what I know.

ANSWER: I think we're getting somewhere important. Your countertransference is a powerful force here but it's acting as an obstacle rather than being useful. The divorce process appears to have precipitated a group regression. We see it in the father, the mother, and in Andy, but now we also see it in you. I won't speak for the lawyers but I wouldn't be surprised if they too regress when faced with these painful and destructive breakups of family life.

If you look carefully at your statement about being too angry and overwhelmed by this situation to be able to use what you know, you'll see that it yields a gold mine of information. It's a perfect example of what Sandler (1976) writes about in his article "Countertransference and Role-Responsiveness." By being reduced to a state of helplessness you are in fact joining the parents who are also too upset and angry to hold on to what they know. Each in his own way is too demanding, too needy, too messy, and you want them to go away and leave you alone. Their expressions of helplessness cause you to react in kind. You are reflecting how they feel. If you look at it from that perspective you can harness your countertransference for the purpose of insight and restore your professional attitude of observing and analyzing both your patients and yourself. With that in place you should have a better chance of reaching the father and reminding him that you're there to help, not hurt. And this vantage point should also help you limit the mother's demands on you. She has her own therapist and that's who can help her look more deeply into the meaning this experience has for her and help her deal with her panic reactions.

QUESTION: That's helpful. It's felt as if these parents were behaving like children screaming for the sun and the moon and things beyond my control, and here I was working hard to be helpful and my efforts were unnoticed and dismissed; in fact I was actually threatened with being fired. Realizing all this I can identify the feeling this evoked in me. I felt wounded. I've been experiencing vague memories from some early time in my life, memories so vague they're mainly of an affective state, rather than events or content of any sort. I know they're evoked by my distress over this case. I guess there's much advantage to being in treatment while doing treatment. When I was in my own therapy I was more able to identify and explore my countertransference. I wouldn't have reached this state of helplessness while in my own treatment.

But tell me, what about the lawyers? What do I do with them? They're not my patients so I don't have to struggle with my countertransference where they're concerned, do I?

ANSWER: There are no limits on who evokes countertransferential responses. Look, these lawyers are making requests of you. You have to decide what to do with these requests and if thinking it through proves very difficult and complicated, you have to assume that your ability to think clearly is bogged down by conflict, that it evokes issues that reach beyond the manifest requests of these lawyers.

QUESTION: What is my obligation to deal with lawyers?

ANSWER: The phrasing of your question implies that you have one. Tell me, who is it who determines something like that?

QUESTION: Well, I do, but I'm glad you posed the question. I had forgotten that it's up to me. I was behaving as if it was up to some other force, somewhere way beyond my authority. I was behaving as if I have an obligation to the lawyers, but I don't. They have their job to do and I have mine. If they think I can make their job easier for them, they'll ask for my help. They don't necessarily understand what therapy is all about. Nor do they understand that my getting involved with them could be harmful rather than helpful. They're doing their job, just as I'm doing mine, but our roles are not necessarily complementary, although ideally they should be.

ANSWER: How could your involvement with them prove to be harmful?

QUESTION: Many ways. Neither parent is particularly stable. Of the two the mother is the more dependable parent. The father's lawyer certainly would not want me to say anything like that, nor would the mother's lawyer want to hear that she's not particularly stable. Then there's the risk that anything I say to the lawyers will polarize the parents, make them feel as if I'm taking sides, upset the working alliance, and possibly precipitate termination. For instance, there's a request from the mother for an affidavit stating that the child should not sleep at his father's house on school nights. I don't disagree with the idea that sleeping in his own bed on school nights is probably preferable for a little boy his age, but on the other hand I don't think it would make a huge difference if he did sleep at his father's house on an occasional school night. I say occasional because this father would not be likely to want his son there often. He travels a lot, works late a lot, and takes customers out to dinner a lot. The sleeping over on school nights is probably just one of those power plays that comes with losing the natural rhythm of family life, of coming and going and seeing your child at will. As for my writing an affidavit curtailing the father's time with his son, I can't think of anything more destructive to my already shaky standing with him than to get involved in that way.

ANSWER: Well, for someone who doesn't know what her obligation to the lawyers is, you certainly figured it out fast once you put your mind to it. How did you do that? Do you know?

QUESTION: When you asked me who determines what my obligations to lawyers is, I was at first startled. It felt as if my observing ego had taken a leave of absence. Then, as I began to focus on your question, it came back. Instead of just reacting, I was able to think and reason and really deal with the situation. What a relief!

ANSWER: I imagine it must be, but you know, you're not alone in becoming confused in a situation such as this combative divorce. Divorce is, for many of us, a trigger word that evokes fear and dread or disapproval. More so if we've had personal experience with it but even if we haven't, it evokes sadness, pain, anxiety, rage, shame, helplessness, and feelings of being abandoned. Even a telephone call from a lawyer can have that kind of trigger effect on us. After all, a battle is going on and lawyers are authority figures who are actively involved in the battle. All sorts of primitive fantasies and fears can be evoked by this volatile situation. Some people, and therapists are no exception, have strong reactions when their authority is questioned and they respond with hostility. Others may be intimidated, resort to passive surrender, and have difficulty in remembering that they too have authority.

Let's be clear about something of enormous importance. *The therapist is and must always be in charge of defining, protecting, and facilitating the therapeutic process.* You momentarily forgot this was your prime responsibility; you had a minor lapse but then recovered your professional identity.

I remember an incident a long time ago that serves as an example of the damage that can result when we fail to protect the treatment process. What happened was this. I was asked to write an affidavit on behalf of a divorcing mother whose husband wanted to be consulted about any and every decision regarding the children. He had gotten furious at his wife because she took their son to an emergency room in the middle of the night without clearing it with him first. His son had gone to the bathroom and on the way had fallen over a toy fire engine and had badly cut his chin. Despite the urgency for medical attention due to his son's loss of blood and need for stitches, this father raged over not being consulted. Compounding the unreasonableness of his position was the fact that he was staying that night at the home of his lady friend and the children's mother would not have been able to reach him even if she had taken the time to try to do so. The father yelled and carried on so that the mother, in despair, asked if I would write an affidavit explaining the importance of making quick decisions in emergencies and not being burdened by having to clear a course of action with a spouse when time was of the essence.

I wrote what I thought was a very sensible and impartial statement saying that it would be in the best interest of both parents if the adult in charge, father or mother, had the right to act without consulting the other parent in the event of an emergency requiring swift action.

The father never forgave me for that letter and his anger was expressed in his not appearing for any of his own scheduled appointments, in the icy tone of voice in which he spoke to me when he occasionally brought his child to my office, and in his not paying his child's bill for several months, until I told him that we would have to discontinue treatment. At that point he must have realized he had gone too far since the child's continuing therapy was mandated by the judge in charge of this case. So, feeling cornered by my refusal to continue without payment and by the fact that this made him look bad to the judge, this father told me he needed a letter from me to the effect that if his son, my patient, did not want to go out with him on a scheduled night, he would nonetheless be allowed to go out with his other child. The letter had no realistic purpose since his wife was very glad her son would not be forced to go out on nights when he preferred to stay home, and had no objection to having her other child, her daughter, visit with her father on those nights. The point was that he had to have a letter from me to save face. If I wrote this meaningless letter for him, he would not feel as powerless and humiliated at not being allowed to fire me and at having to pay my bill. Having his authority as a parent so compromised, he needed to feel that he too could make conditions.

You were much wiser than I was in realizing that writing an affidavit would cause harm rather than provide help. I was too identified with the mother to use good judgment and made the all-too-common mistake of temporarily leaving my role as therapist and entering a different realm.

The reason I think this a particularly good example is that on the surface my actions appear quite reasonable. An impasse between the parents had been reached, I wrote an impartial letter to help settle this impasse, and so forth.

Had I been other than the child's therapist it would have been an appropriate action, but in this situation I was a transferential figure to these parents and my writing that letter was tantamount to saying that I loved the mother more than the father. So what appeared to be born out of good common sense, an expedient action, turned out to have a countertransferential element that the father did not fail to grasp.

You mentioned earlier that being in your own therapy might have significantly helped in identifying and working with your countertransference. Often we can identify our countertransference despite not being in our own treatment, but when we find that our countertransference *frequently* goes unanalyzed, that's a good reason to return to our own treatment and do some additional work on ourselves.

QUESTION: I'm aware of that and do think about it sometimes. I know I will go back to treatment at some point; I don't know what will lead me back there, but something about work or the rest of my life eventually will.

But I want to talk a bit about my work with the child in this divorce situation, my patient Andy. He never talks about the divorce. His father moved out one month ago and has an apartment nearby. Andy spends weekends at his father's apartment and only sees his parents together when he's picked up and delivered to one of their homes. At those times the parents are curt and unfriendly towards each other. All in all there have been dramatic changes in Andy's life, both in terms of living arrangements and atmosphere.

Andy is happy to come to his sessions and plays with his favorite toys as before. He includes me in the fantasies he makes up about the animals, the soldiers, and the cowboys and Indians. He always portrays me as someone who makes order. Sometimes I'm the nurse or doctor who takes care of the wounded soldiers. Sometimes I'm the farmer who feeds the animals. Sometimes I'm the peacemaker who tells the cowboys and Indians to be friends and not fight. Sometimes he has cars crashing and I'm the cop who restores order. But he never talks about the divorce. Should I bring it up? Should I suggest he play with some of the family dolls rather than with the toys of his choosing? I feel as if I'm colluding with his denial of the situation.

ANSWER: Why do you tell me he's avoiding the topic of divorce and then substantiate your statement with examples that sound to me as if all he talks about is divorce related?

QUESTION: Oh my! How did I miss that? Of course! All his play is about fighting, and I'm always the restorer of peace and order. Now I'm a little embarrassed. How did I get so concrete?

ANSWER: There's no doubt that your general discomfort with this subject has a lot to do with your concreteness. But now that you've recognized the theme of his communication, how would you approach his games? What would you say to him?

QUESTION: I could say he seems very interested in fighting and then settling the fight. He likes me to be the peacemaker. Could he tell me a little more about it, about why this is so interesting and important to him?

ANSWER: That sounds good. It's tactful, it's to the point, but it doesn't rush him or intrude. What kind of response would you expect?

QUESTION: I would expect him to say, "Come on, let's just play." At least that's what I'm afraid he might say.

ANSWER: Why afraid? What would you want him to say that he isn't saying?

QUESTION: He isn't saying that his mommy and daddy are getting a divorce, that they seem to hate each other, that he hates to see their angry faces and mean-sounding way of speaking. That he doesn't know what's going to happen and he's scared because his mother cries all the time and talks on the phone and whispers when he comes into the room and tells him to go into another room because she needs "privacy." And his daddy always looks as if he's going to yell except when he's with this lady he calls Nina. Then he smiles and laughs a lot and tells him to go play in another room.

Andy isn't saying he wants me to fix all this so it can be the way it was when he was little and people weren't angry all the time, but the wish must be there somewhere.

ANSWER: You allowed yourself to fantasize about Andy's world and the place you have in it. That can be a useful exercise, but it's important to remember that you've embellished his play and directed the theme to fit the drama of his life *as you see it*. So this creation is partly yours and only partly coming from him.

QUESTION: But would you disagree that he would like his world to be restored to the way it was before his parents split up?

ANSWER: I don't know the answer. What do we really know about the way it was? Maybe it was full of fighting and tension even then. Maybe in the past Andy wished his father would go away because he was afraid of him, or because his mother was afraid of him. Maybe Andy, who is of oedipal age, wanted his mother to himself. I could go on speculating, but you know enough about the personality structure of these three people and about their history to have some idea of the way things might have been before the divorce. But you also know that being egocentric is the norm for little children, so they tend to think they're responsible for all sorts of matters that have little to do with them. You know that if Andy, in his oedipal fantasies, did indeed wish his father gone, the father's departure would be all the more frightening if he believed it to be the realization of his wish. Also, since these wishes are rarely completely one-sided, Andy's wish for the father's disappearance would have coexisted with the wish for his continued presence as a strong and protective force in his life and an object for identification.

So, while you consider the external changes imposed by the divorce situation, you must also pay equal attention to the internal conflicts this child might be grappling with and that are being expressed in his play. Is he looking for your help as peacemaker for his parents, or does he want your help in finding intrapsychic peace?

It's important to look at a child's external reality without losing sight of the inter- and intrasystemic reactions stimulated by reality. One of the problems of overidentifying with your patient is that it obscures the big picture.

QUESTION: Could you give me an example of how I might be losing sight of the big picture by identifying with Andy?

ANSWER: If Andy did indeed have hostile wishes towards his dad and wanted him to be banished from the home, and if he believes his father's departure to be the result of these wishes, this belief could cause him intense suffering and also terror at being so powerful. If you, on the other hand, are assuming that his distress is primarily in regard to the actual separation of his parents, you're missing a very big part of the story he's telling you in his play.

QUESTION: That makes a lot of sense. Would you also explain the difference between intersystemic and intrasystemic conflict?

ANSWER: An intersystemic conflict is a conflict between the psychic institutions, between id, ego, and superego. An intrasystemic conflict is a conflict within one of the psychic institutions, as for instance a conflict within the ego.

QUESTION: How would some of these conflicts be manifested in a young child? Can you give me an example?

ANSWER: An intersystemic conflict in a young child could take place when ego-powered (aggressive) strivings to be big, independent, and autonomous clash with the id (libidinal) drive to be a baby, helpless, taken care of, and gratified. The manifestation of this conflict can take many forms, such as extreme bossiness at home alternating with acute separation anxiety at nursery school.

An intrasystemic conflict could be a conflict within the ego, such as, for example, a conflict between the realization of ambition and the ego ideal of modesty. This sort of conflict in a young child could be manifested by getting the lead in the class play and getting sick the day of the performance, or by a pattern of underachievement punctuated by flashes of excellence.

QUESTION: Well, that's helpful. If the kind of self-sabotage you describe occurred to a child of divorcing parents, I would have been more likely to see it as related to the divorce upheaval. It's good to be reminded that there's a lot going on beneath the surface.

ANSWER: But it's also important to remember that it's not one or the other. Divorce is a major upheaval that triggers a great deal of upset and also exacerbates psychic trends and patterns particular to the psychic structures of the individuals involved. This obviously applies to the principal players, the members of the family. But it also reverberates beyond the boundaries of the immediate family and leaves its mark on people in the periphery. Teachers, nannies, friends, relatives, and therapists are all drawn in, to the degree of their vulnerability, to drastic change and loss. Our job grows very complex under these circumstances and taps our deepest reservoirs of strength, talent, and tact.

12

✌

Some Typical Dilemmas in Work with Parents

QUESTION: What do you do when parents make requests that you feel obliged to refuse because they're inappropriate? How do you manage to say "no" to such demands and maintain a good working relationship with the parents?

ANSWER: Sometimes that's not so easy to achieve and sometimes you fail no matter how tactful you are. Nonetheless you can't agree to inappropriate demands. But let's get more specific about what you consider to be inappropriate. Give me some examples, please.

QUESTION: Here's something that happened to me very recently. A mother brought her 8-year-old daughter Melissa to her usual weekly appointment, but on this date she brought Scott, her 4-year-old son, as well. She told me that Scott would have to join us for Melissa's session while she ran out to do errands. I told her that I couldn't allow that; Melissa needed to have her regular session, and that meant just the two of us. Mrs. M. shook her head and in an icy tone told me her little boy would then have to wait in the waiting room alone while she ran out to do some food shopping. She said she didn't think that forty-five minutes alone in a strange waiting room was a very nice situation to place a 4-year-old in, but since I wouldn't let him into the office, and the weather was bad, and he was getting over a cold, she had to choose that over the other unfortunate alternatives of exposing him to a drafty supermarket or staying in the waiting room with him and having no food in the house.

I said I was sorry but she could not leave Scott in the waiting room unattended. Couldn't she stay with him and find a way to do her supermarket shopping later? Melissa's mother got even angrier, and grabbing Scott's hand said, "If I had that alternative I wouldn't be having this conversation with you! But I can see I'm not going to get any cooperation from you. I guess you missed school on the day they taught your class that you're supposed to *help* people, not make their lives more difficult!" With Scott's hand in hers she stormed out of the office and slammed the door behind her.

I was stunned, angry, very worried about the effect of this exchange on Melissa, and very concerned about the future of my relationship with this mother. I had a sense of dread about it, as if a rift had been created that could never be mended.

This all happened yesterday and I've thought about it a lot, but I haven't done anything about it yet. I think I should call Melissa's mother and discuss the incident, don't you think so?

ANSWER: Yes, I do think so. It's a great example of the kind of difficult situations child therapists find themselves in. The incident you described is not unusual in the treatment of children. It's the type of thing that happens when one or both parents resent the therapist and the treatment situation.

Let's spend some time on this example and learn as much as we can from it. Then we'll develop some general principles that will help us in situations of this sort, situations wherein a parent makes a request we have to refuse, with the consequence of our refusal placing the future of the treatment in jeopardy.

Tell me, what is Melissa's mother like? What diagnostic formulation did you make about her at the end of the evaluation process?

QUESTION: I didn't arrive at a diagnostic formulation. I had noted that this mother is always impatient, edgy, and angry but I hadn't organized my thinking to take these observations further and use them diagnostically to aid my understanding of this mother. I had placed all my concentration and effort on Melissa. I guess I was drawn to Melissa because she's such a frightened, unhappy child, a lost soul if ever there was one. I guess my concern about the child overrode any interest I might have had in the mother. But let me backtrack a bit and give you some history of how the referral came about.

Melissa was referred for treatment by her school principal. She's a third grader. She began attending her current school in kindergarten. Each year her teachers expressed concern at her lack of vitality, her apparent lack of investment in learning, and her lack of interest in interacting with the other children. She hasn't tried to make friends, nor do children pay attention to her. Her sole and constant interest is drawing and she's very good at that.

Each year her teachers have expressed their concern about her to her mother. They consider Melissa to be a depressed and isolated child. On several occasions they've suggested that Mrs. M. take her to see a therapist and have her evaluated regarding the appropriateness of psychotherapy. Mrs. M. ignored these suggestions until the principal stepped in and was quite insistent that the mother follow up on these recommendations and consult a child therapist.

Although Melissa's mother was very much against seeking professional help, once the principal gave her my name and told her to be sure to call me, Mrs. M. did call. After a brief evaluation I recommended treatment. Mrs. M. was obviously distressed by the idea of treatment, but since the school had insisted she follow up on my recommendation, she complied.

So you see it's against this mother's wishes that I work with Melissa. At first it was against Melissa's wishes as well, but now, after six months of weekly appointments, Melissa has made a good connection with me and looks forward to her sessions.

Mrs. M. is always brusque with me but she brings Melissa every week, then runs off to do errands, and is always back in time to pick her up. This was the first time she brought her son along and made the unexpected and inappropriate request I described. She treated me as if I were a baby-sitter or a neighbor, don't you agree?

ANSWER: Yes, but then let's take that a little further and ask how you felt about being seen as a baby-sitter or neighbor?

QUESTION: I was very much offended, of course.

ANSWER: Why were you offended, and why the "of course"?

QUESTION: I'm a little surprised by your question. I'm a psychotherapist, not a baby-sitter or a neighbor. I'm a trained professional. I like to be recognized as such. Wouldn't you be offended if you were seen as a baby-sitter or neighbor?

ANSWER: I might be, but if I found myself having such a strong reaction, I would hope that an inner alarm would sound, alerting me to danger. By danger I refer to the temporary loss of my professional grounding. Hopefully the alarm would mobilize my work ego and help me understand my reaction from a countertransferential perspective.

We must always remember that people assign roles to us, and whatever the role, it's important to pay attention, note what's transpiring, and try to understand what's being enacted. We need to study the role we've been given, the interaction that follows, and our response to the interaction. Paying attention to how we handle the role we've been given is a good way of learning something about our patients and ourselves.

Earlier I mentioned Sandler's article on the valuable use of countertransference in this specific sense, in the awareness of the role we've been assigned by the patient and our response to it. What you need to do with Melissa's mother is to stop yourself from just reacting to her and ask yourself why you got so upset. For instance, what was it about being viewed as similar to a baby-sitter that felt so demeaning to you? What, after all, is a baby-sitter? Isn't a baby-sitter a person hired by the parent to perform the important function of caring for her child? True, sitters are not necessarily as educated as are psychotherapists, nor is the care they give of the same order and purpose, but they're caregivers just as we are. Do you think this mother necessarily understands the difference between a baby-sitter and a psychotherapist?

Look, there are two lines of inquiry that require your attention here. One line requires reviewing your contacts with Melissa's mother from the beginning, from the first phone call, and arriving at a diagnostic understanding of her. That means taking all your observations, all the descriptive terms you use about her, and translating them into a psychodynamic understanding of this woman.

The second line of inquiry has to do with understanding your own reactions. It's fine to be proud of your credentials and status as a psychotherapist, but if your interaction with this mother made you feel so vulnerable, so stripped of your professional identity, something is going on within you that really requires some self-analysis. Melissa's mother really got you frazzled and not only in regard to your professional status. It sounds as if you experienced her as making herself big and making you small. Would you agree with that?

QUESTION: Yes, and this is making me very uncomfortable. Now that you mentioned "big" and "small" I recognize having felt small in this situation. And it is peculiar of me to feel so easily reduced in stature. I hadn't really considered that aspect of it. I was behaving as if Mrs. M. really had the power to make me small. How come I let myself be so reduced? I guess this is a really clear example of how powerful a part is played by countertransference. I can see that Mrs. M., at some point, stopped being the mother of my young patient and became someone in my own past. This is beginning to feel very familiar. I hate to admit it but it was always very easy for my siblings to make me feel as if I was "less than." I guess that point of vulnerability doesn't go away completely. Look at how it resurfaced with Mrs. M.

What do I do with this insight now that I have it, and how do I make sure I don't miss it next time something like this happens?

ANSWER: Now that you've recognized the countertransferential element you can continue to analyze it, but at the same time you can concentrate on the other line of inquiry I suggested, and that is to try to understand this mother. Dealing with your countertransference will free you to view this mother from a professional perspective rather than from a rivalrous one.

Let me remind you of an earlier conversation (p. 18) we had in which I referred to the following principle: The child's therapist has to stand equidistant to child and parents. Only when positioned that way can the therapist be alert to all the subtle shifts of affect and behavior that inform and guide our work.

One of the problems you ran into with this case is the most common pitfall of child treatment. You did not position yourself equidistant to mother and child. Instead you overidentified with Melissa and her mother became an intruder, a second-class citizen. The fact that this mother is antagonistic to treatment and rather unpleasant to you makes it all too easy to view her as the enemy, but we can't allow ourselves to let that happen when occupying our professional place. I am making a strong distinction between how we might react to hostility in our private lives and how we deal with it as therapists. In our private lives we can of course just react to unpleasant behavior like anyone else; in our professional role we might also react, but then we try to understand our reaction while at the same time trying to understand what lies behind a patient's antagonism.

I don't mean to imply that we always succeed in being so even-handed and objective in our role as therapists. We don't. Sometimes we lack the energy to be so alert and vigilant. Sometimes we find a parent particularly difficult or so hostile that we just react as we might outside our office. Sometimes that can happen during an initial session, and, despite the most scrupulous self-analysis, become immutable. When upon reflection we think our response is too complex for a timely resolution, we're better off not taking the case on.

But I don't think it was that bad between you and Mrs. M. Am I right?

QUESTION: It wasn't quite that bad, but in retrospect I see I avoided the bad feeling she had towards me and towards treatment in general. I just wanted to get to work with that sad little girl. How could I have addressed her antagonism towards treatment?

ANSWER: The answer is so obvious you'll be surprised at having asked the question. I'm just going to turn it back to you and ask you to think of how you would approach such a situation with an adult who is consulting you for treatment for himself and simultaneously expressing contempt and disdain for treatment.

QUESTION: You're right, I do find that much easier. I would ask such a patient about the disdain. I would explore it with him, try to learn whether it was based on his having had some bad experiences with other therapists, or whether bad experiences with therapists had affected family members, or whether the hostility had a less concrete base, not so much the result of experience but of such matters as fear, suspicion, paranoia, a sense of humiliation at needing help . . . or all of the above.

ANSWER: Why would you know what to do with an adult who is your patient but not with an adult who is the mother of your patient?

QUESTION: A point well taken, and we've been here before. Everything that's gone wrong with Melissa's mother has been the result of my not allowing her to be a person in her own right. I didn't pay attention to her as an important part of Melissa's treatment. I gave her short shrift. Now I'm going to try to salvage the situation. I'm going to get to know this woman and try to connect with her and see how I can help her as well as her daughter. Do you think it's too late, that too much damage was done?

ANSWER: That remains to be seen. But before we forget, I want to come back to a question I asked you earlier that might help you. I asked whether you thought Mrs. M. really understood the difference between a baby-sitter and a therapist. Do you think she does?

QUESTION: **Well, as you pointed out before, we both have caretaking functions, but is it possible that anyone living in this day and age would have trouble distinguishing between a therapist and a baby-sitter?**

ANSWER: Sure, I agree. It does seems unlikely that anyone living in this day and age, in our culture, could blur the difference between therapist and baby-sitter. So, as a therapist, what do you do when someone seems confused about this very obvious difference? Please note that I asked what you do as a *therapist*, for you might respond to these situations differently in your personal life, your life outside of work, than in your professional life. In your personal life you might respond with surprise, disbelief, annoyance, and so forth. But in your professional role you take such apparent confusion in a patient as a signal, and you become very interested in what has just happened. You recognize that the confusion, whatever its base, is an important piece of information about this person.

This a good example of the trouble we get into when we treat the parents of our child patients as if they somehow were outside the therapeutic environment that we live in while we work, as if they remained outside the boundaries of an attitude we must enter and uphold in order to be able to do our work.

Mrs. M. might be a very needy person, whose hunger for being taken care of is ego dystonic or unacceptable on some other level. If this is so, she appears to defend against her hunger for care by assuming a rather harsh and off-putting manner. If she were your *primary* patient you probably would have registered this trait in her a long time ago and understood it to be a defensive maneuver. But because she is the *mother* of your patient, you did not view this and other irritating traits as diagnostically important. This omission is a typical failing of child therapists. To counter this common failing we have to be very disciplined about doing a diagnostic assessment of the parents. It helps us maintain a professional attitude about parents and prevents us from reacting to them in a social manner. I suggest that when that social manner enters our consulting room, some form of countertransference is being expressed.

I want to explore this situation a little more. What do you think might have been different from the beginning had you questioned the reason for Mrs. M.'s cool and distancing manner?

QUESTION: Well, now that you mention it, had I even thought of questioning her attitude, I probably would have wondered what she was defending against by pushing me away, by being so unfriendly.

ANSWER: So possibly you might have wondered whether a needy and frightened child lived inside that off-putting manner of hers.

QUESTION: Yes, but instead I seem to have skipped thinking about it altogether. Since I viewed her as the unpleasant parent of a very sad and deprived little girl, and since in my heart I held her responsible for her child's unhappiness, my ability to connect with her was doomed. I didn't even try. It seemed hopeless. But had I been sensitive to her unhappiness and her need for help, I would have proceeded very differently.

ANSWER: It's likely that Mrs. M. pushes away the help and connections she craves. Do you think she's aware of wanting something from you?

QUESTION: Probably not consciously, but when she wanted me to take care of her little boy, that was her way of asking for help, wasn't it?

ANSWER: Yes. Could it mean she was beginning to trust you just a little? You see, you're in a difficult situation with Mrs. M. She guards her neediness carefully and you have to respect her defense. It's there for reasons you know nothing about, but you can be sure she's been through a lot to be so brittle and angry and suspicious. So, how do you form an alliance with her without intruding on her determination to be super self-sufficient?

QUESTION: I find that kind of patient very difficult, even when it's an adult coming for herself. But at least then the patient is admitting she wants help. But when it's a parent, I really don't know how to approach that person. How do you do that? It seems to me the stakes are different when it's the parent of a child. What if you make a serious blunder and the parent pulls the child out of treatment because of it?

ANSWER: Of course that can happen, and does happen regularly. But if you understand the situation and take the information you have and let it guide you, you are less likely to make a serious blunder.

QUESTION: Could you expand on that and give me an approach to Mrs. M. that would help me? For instance, I have to call her and try to salvage the situation. Do you have any suggestions of what I could say to her now, knowing what you know about how angry she was at my last session with Melissa?

ANSWER: First of all, don't assume you know how angry she is at you now that a day or two have passed. This is not idle reassurance on my part. I mean you *really* don't know. She might be angrier than you can imagine or she might be less angry and more concerned about her own behavior that day. So the first order of business is to make no assumptions. If you can do that, your tone will reflect it, and that's a good start.

I would call Mrs. M. and tell her you're very sorry not to have been able to be meet her request the other day. I would ask her whether Scott was over his cold. If the conversation seemed to be going okay thus far, I would tell her that the incident of the other day made you realize you had not discussed certain aspects of treatment with her and you would like to set up an appointment with her and explain why it was so important not to change the conditions of Melissa's appointment in any way. This meeting with her would also allow you to have a general discussion about Melissa. You could tell her you were eager to learn how Melissa is doing at home and at school, to hear her general observations of her daughter. You would also like to discuss some of your observations of Melissa and see if she shares them.

What I'm suggesting is very simple but it conveys that the two of you are partners where Melissa is concerned. While what I've suggested is really plain common sense, it's also a cautious approach insofar as it doesn't open anything up over the phone that would be better addressed in person. But it's a little difficult for me to present a one-sided imaginary conversation. Naturally, Mrs. M.'s responses would affect how you would proceed.

Of course I'm wondering what happened to the father. You've never mentioned him, but that's a whole other subject.

QUESTION: Well, I'm struck by your suggestion that I say I'm sorry for not being able to oblige her requests. That would not have occurred to me since I found her request inappropriate. But I get your point, I think. My finding her request inappropriate should have alerted me to the possibility that Mrs. M. might have misunderstood something about my role as Melissa's therapist. Or perhaps it was something quite different. Perhaps it was the emergence of her wish that I help her, give to her, take care of her. Or perhaps it was both of the above . . . and all the other possible factors that I haven't learned about yet. In light of what we're saying, an apology makes sense to me.

ANSWER: *When a therapist finds the behavior of a child, or parent, or any patient inappropriate, that's a red alert, a signal that the therapist needs to analyze his reaction. Very often we use the word "inappropriate" when our normal anticipatory system has been jolted, when something unexpected has happened. It's fine to react strongly to the unanticipated and take note. It's not so fine if we give the action that unsettled us a pejorative label and dismiss it as such. In our work, the appearance of what we might call "inappropriate" provides an opportunity for examining and deepening our diagnostic thinking. Often the appearance of unexpected behavior in our patients can serve as a catalyst to opening our ability to understand them more fully.* I think you understand what I'm saying very well and came to the same conclusion.

QUESTION: Yes, after you got me to stop and think, I did. You also asked me about Melissa's father and why I've never mentioned him. Nobody knows anything about him. Mrs. M. lives alone with her two children and there has never been any mention of a father. When I asked her to tell me about Melissa's father during the consultation phase she said that that was a closed subject and one she would never discuss. She told me Melissa and Kevin had her and nobody else in the world, and that was all I needed to know.

ANSWER: Well, at some point, when the time seems right, you might tell her you remember that this is a subject she doesn't want to talk about, and of course you respect that, but it would help you a lot if she would tell you what Melissa knows about her father and whether she ever talks about him or expresses any feelings about him.

The Melissa situation has been a useful example of the type of difficulty we encounter in child treatment. You presented this incident to illustrate your question about the child's therapist refusing to comply with a demand made by a parent that was inappropriate. In this case the inappropriate request was made by a mother with whom you had not established a working alliance, a mother who was angry about her child being in treatment. Countertransferential issues got in your way, making it hard to think clearly and objectively.

Can you think of any other requests from parents that come up that you find yourself having to refuse?

QUESTION: Oh, yes. Parents sometimes expect me to attend events in the child's life. For example, I'm sometimes invited to graduations, plays in which the child has a part, bar mitzvahs, even birthday parties. Sometimes parents have trouble understanding why I refuse. Sometimes my child patients also have trouble understanding why I refuse.

ANSWER: Why do you refuse?

QUESTION: I want to keep the therapy in the office. That's where I think it belongs. I think that's better for the patient and for me. Do you disagree?

ANSWER: No, I agree, but not everyone agrees with us. There are therapists who attend some of these family functions and have their list of reasons for doing so. Let's try to understand more fully our position on this. Tell me your thinking.

QUESTION: Well, I'm the therapist; I'm involved with the family in a very specific way. My role is professional. I don't talk about myself or reveal information about my personal life or my family situation. I feel that keeping the relationship in the office is consistent with my general attitude of having a very specific function and not spilling it into a social situation. Would you agree with that?

ANSWER: Very much so, but I would take it even further. *Our work is very demanding. Maintaining a professional attitude all day long, no matter how we feel, how tired we are, how difficult the patient might be, how charged the atmosphere might get, is hard work. And our work doesn't end when we leave our offices. We think about our patients when we're not with them. We write up session notes, some of us go to supervision, attend ongoing case and theoretical seminars and lectures, and keep up with our reading. To become involved in the social life of our patients is not only questionable on their account, it's questionable on our account. We need time for our private lives.*

Now that I've said all this I will add that sometimes very unusual circumstances might come up that cause us to make an exception to this position. I would just be very careful to understand why we might be tempted to make an exception. By careful, I mean giving care to understanding our own motives thoroughly before taking action.

QUESTION: What about a parent asking you to read a popular parenting book to see if you agree with the advice given by the author? I have so little time, I really don't feel like reading pop culture books. What would your position be on that kind of request?

ANSWER: I agree with the idea that we don't particularly want our patients, and/or the parents of children we treat to give us reading assignments. But I would be very interested in exploring the request, learning what it was really about.

QUESTION: Could you give me an illustration of how you would go about doing that?

ANSWER: Well, for example, there are many popular books on handling a range of problems including that of children who have difficulty going to sleep and staying asleep. Many of the parents who have consulted me about sleeping problems had read various books on the subject. Some parents swore by them, even though their toddlers, or 3- or 4-year-old children were still up till all hours of the night and the book they held in such esteem had failed to help them. And here they were now, in my office, hoping for help from me. Other parents disliked the books, tried to resolve their child's sleep problems on their own, and were unable to do so. And although these parents didn't approve of the methods suggested in these books, they still were eager for me to read them to see what I thought.

While I haven't read most of these self-help books I have read two written by psychoanalysts (Schwartzman 1990, Siegler 1994) and, as you might expect, their focus is on sensitizing parents to pay careful attention to their children: to listen, to observe, and to think about what's being communicated. These books are not prescriptive; rather, they encourage taking care in the best possible way.

What I've learned from listening to parents talk about other self-help books is that the books offer a structure, a method, a prescription for how to do something they couldn't do on their own. Now it's possible that these books offer a lot more than that. I'm limiting my statement to what parents typically focus on in these discussions. Some parents welcomed the structure recommended by these books and others rejected it, yet both groups wanted me to read the books.

I find this very interesting. Why would some parents take so much comfort in the fact that putting a child to sleep was difficult for many other parents and such a common difficulty that books were written on it? And why would other parents dislike being portrayed as members of a group that have this difficulty?

What I find fascinating is this. Why do some parents need so much instruction in putting a young child to sleep? Why would certain parents insist that their child is so special that ordinary rules, like a specific bedtime, cannot apply?[10] These are important questions for the therapist to consider. They give direction to the kind of exploration one might pursue with parents who have insecurities around taking charge, being the ones who set the tone and present their child with firm and clear expectations.

QUESTION: What else did you learn from the parents who didn't like the books?

ANSWER: In the case of the sleep problem I just referred to, I learned that the mother was horrified by the idea of a unilateral demand being made on her child, even though the demand was that her child go to sleep at a particular hour and stay asleep all night. She saw such an expectation and its enforcement as cruel. However, upon exploring this attitude, I discovered she believed that hers was a *special* child and her reason for seeking the consultation was for me to convince her husband that they should not expect their little girl to abide by something so ordinary and commonplace as rules and regulations about sleep. Discovering the mother's fantasy about having a special child gave me a lot of help in understanding how to proceed with her.

In my general contacts with parents who referred to self-help books I found certain patterns. Often, the parents who disliked the self-help-book approach to sleep problems did

---

10. See Siskind (1992), Chapter 7, for a full description of a case of a child with a sleep problem.

not want to enforce anything on their child. These parents did not believe in taking charge. They wanted a democracy with everyone having an equal voice. It's very helpful to our work to understand that type of parental position. It gives us a very clear idea of where the problem originates and how to approach it.

Many of the parents who liked the books admired the idea of having definite expectations of their child and having a routine that's adhered to, but they were unable to enforce this type of order into their family life. When we learn that parents wish to take charge but find they can't do it, we're faced with a situation that's very different from one where the parents object to the notion of being the ones to take charge. It makes a big difference to our work to know which of these positions we're addressing.

So, to answer your question, I don't run out and buy and read the books my patients or the parents of my patients recommend, but I do ask them to tell me what they would like me to have learned from these books. What was it about a particular book that was important to them?

You know, this happens as much with adult patients as with the parents of child patients. There are a lot of popular self-help books that get recommended to therapists. These recommendations are always interesting and their exploration useful. The patient who wants us to read a particular book is always expressing a transferential wish that can range anywhere from wanting to be more present in the therapist's life outside the office, to a desire for a collegial relationship, or other issues along competitive lines such as devaluing the therapist, saying the therapist is superfluous, replaceable by a book, and so forth. My point is that reading the book is not necessary, but exploring the request is very productive. If you ask to be told what they want you to know about the book and take it from there, it's making very good use of the request.

QUESTION: I suppose the same attitude could be taken about movies, television programs, or plays. Sometimes parents will ask me whether I think a particular program is appropriate for their 5-year-old, or they've learned that their 8-year-old was taken to see a very inappropriate movie and want me to see it to help them find a way of wiping away any damage it might have done. I guess exploring their request is the more useful way to go in these situations as well.

ANSWER: Not only is it more useful, but in these situations you're being enticed to be smarter, wiser, and bigger than the parent. If you accept that role you're in trouble. You aren't smarter and wiser; you're trained in a particular area. Stick to your area, and help the parents find ways of strengthening theirs.

13

✧

What Do We Do When Parents Can't Cope, Demand Advice, Have Values That Clash with Ours, Don't Pay Their Bills . . . ?

QUESTION: I understand that it's not our role to give advice to parents, but what if a parent has poor judgment, lacks ordinary common sense, and is truly inadequate? Some parents we see might even be mentally retarded. We see parents whose ability to think clearly and function adequately is marginal. If we have knowledge that could help a parent who is unable to understand his child, a parent who just doesn't know what to do in the most basic situations, and that parent asks for our help, shouldn't we provide that help?

ANSWER: That's a very good question, and the way you raised it contains some of the answer. You see, you made a diagnostic statement about this hypothetical parent. You described the person as having poor judgment and lacking common sense. Now let's examine what poor judgment and lack of common sense tell us about a person. We're talking about two very important ego functions; a deficit in these ego functions has wide-ranging implications. Judgment and common sense develop out of reality testing and reality awareness, which in turn depend on the development of very early ego functions, such as anticipation, memory, and delay. Object relations and identity formation are part of this developmental schema, as is the ability to synthesize and integrate.

So as you know, a person whose judgment is seriously impaired and who lacks common sense is manifesting serious deficiency in achievement of the kind of ego functioning that's essential to being a parent. Then you add lack of intelligence, which may be part of the person's genetic makeup, or it may be pseudo-stupidity born out of conflict, or it may be the manifestation of a very primitive, possibly psychotic personality that cannot observe and process the way the rest of us do. So what do you do when a parent like that asks you how to toilet train his child, or how much sleep his child needs, or what to do when his toddler refuses her bath, or what to do when his son bites other children?

The first thing you do is consider arranging for that parent to get at least as much help as his child is receiving. You either work with that parent on a weekly basis in addition to working with his child, or you refer that parent to another therapist who is capable of playing the dual role of offering treatment and child guidance, a combined therapeutic objective that requires a lot of skill.

QUESTION: Why do you suggest that child guidance is not a role that every therapist would be capable of providing as part of treatment?

ANSWER: For two reasons. Some therapists still feel that when a patient spends a lot of therapy time talking about his child, that's a form of resistance. This position is kind of old fashioned and not based on sound understanding of diagnosis. Perhaps it originates with a statement that Freud made in which he stated that when a patient speaks exclusively about his love life he is avoiding the broad area of work, and vice versa. Freud's point was that if a patient speaks of only one area of his life it's to avoid other matters of high importance. Of course Freud was referring to patients in analysis five or six times a week who were diagnosed as neurotic. We're presently talking about a patient population that covers a wide range of diagnostic constellations, including some whose psychic structure is much more primitive than that of a neurotic person. We're also talking about a different treatment situation than that of classical psychoanalysis. Nonetheless, some of our colleagues ignore these considerations and stick to a rather old-fashioned point of view about what constitutes manifestations of resistance.

In contrast, some of our enlightened therapists know that for some patients, talking about their child is the only way they can enter the treatment process (Weinstein 1987); it's their visa into self-exploration and eventually self-knowledge. Therapists who have a broader, more evolved perspective understand early development and its vicissitudes. They understand how early developmental derailments can skew subsequent development. These therapists recognize that there are many reasons some patients make their child the focal or even exclusive subject of treatment. In some cases, for instance, when a patient talks about his child he is really talking about aspects of himself. This would not be an example of resistance. This could be an example of lack of differentiation between self- and object representation resulting in an inability to distinguish and recognize the child as a separate person.

So point one is to understand that the treatment of an adult can proceed and be effective even though the patient talks almost exclusively about his child, and that sometimes the exclusivity of this topic persists for a very long time.

Now we come to point two, and that is combining the treatment of an adult who is a parent with some aspects of child guidance. By the way, we should find a better term for this kind of work than *child guidance*. Guidance always connotes something prescriptive and advice giving. I don't mean anything like that, although the idea of guiding or helping a parent navigate through the demands and confusions of parenthood is closer to my point. What I have in mind in this regard is finding interventions that help the parent become more aware of what's going on between him and his child, and more able to observe and reflect their interactions and the feelings they evoke. That's a delicate job and it takes skill to achieve. And yet I mean something very simple. For instance, one could say to a parent who has a lot of trouble putting her child to sleep:

> "Putting Johnny to sleep seems so hard for you that you can't even imagine that there's a way to make it easier. You talk about it as if there was no way of changing the situation. As if it was fixed forever to remain so difficult."

An intervention like that captures the patient's interest and awakens her to realizing what a closed system she's created. It's very different from presenting the more *educational* fact that putting a child to sleep is not an insurmountable task. Do you see the difference between these two statements containing similar information, the first an intervention that gets the patient to do some reflective work, the second the offering of information that demands nothing of the patient and does not build the working alliance?

QUESTION: I do see the difference between the two approaches, and I find that very helpful. But I want to discuss a different kind of situation I'm struggling with. I'd like to describe the mother of one of my young patients. Both parents are what we would diagnostically view as primitive personalities. They both have very little idea of

what to do with a child. Their son, Jack, is 3 years old
and wildly out of control. The father and mother are both
upset about this but the father wants me to deal with his
wife and son and does not want to participate except for
an occasional appointment.

Jack was referred by his day care center. At my initial
meeting with Jack I observed that the mother and the
father, who was present as well, were at their wit's end.
They yelled at Jack and threatened to hit, and he paid no
attention to them. Jack was restless, destructive of my
toys, screamed a lot, and was very hard to contain. I saw
the parents alone the next day and they asked me what
to do about every aspect of Jack's life: what to feed him,
how often to bathe him, about dressing, toileting, safety,
toys, television. They asked for help in stopping his sys-
tematic destruction of toys and furniture. Now this is my
question. With parents who are so unable to cope with
even the most basic elements of care, do I worry about
giving advice? Do I worry about seeming prescriptive or
assuming a role that might make me appear smarter and
wiser than they are?

ANSWER: Do you know what to do with their child?

QUESTION: No. But I know I can learn as I get to know him.
I can learn something just by being with him and observing him.

ANSWER: What's it like to be with him?

QUESTION: At first it was nerve wracking. In one minute
he would knock over a bunch of journals from my shelves
or make a mess wherever he stood with whatever was near
him. I quickly realized I could not use paints or magic
markers with him lest he write all over my walls before I
could stop him. There were other toys as well that were

at risk of being destroyed or becoming destructive. So I "Jack proofed" my office and now when he comes there is very little he can do that's going to damage my room and have me upset with him. With that in place I'm getting to know him. We can now have conversations and I can focus my attention on him rather than on keeping the two of us and the room from getting wrecked.

ANSWER: Where is the mother while Jack is in session with you?

QUESTION: At first his mother was in the room with us, but she couldn't stop talking to him and to me. She talked to him in a very harsh, threatening tone and kept wanting me to commiserate with her on how awful he was. It was definitely not productive, so I decided to have her stay in the waiting room and scheduled separate appointments for her alone. When I'm with her she asks me to tell her how to handle anything and everything and there is no way that I can *not* give her advice. I can't help it. What would you do?

ANSWER: You're describing a very special set of circumstances and that, of course, requires adapting our approach to what this particular situation requires. It appears that you're doing just that. What you're describing confirms the position that a diagnostic assessment of the parent is not only useful but essential. From your observations we might speculate that this is a woman with extreme ego deficits and perhaps a psychotic structure. If that's so, she is truly not equipped to deal with even basic child care. Under such circumstances she would feel lost and helpless, and then her wish that you be a "good object" who will help her and stand by her and not abandon her is growth promoting and should be understood as such. That she would turn to a person for help rather than expressing her frustration and helplessness by turning to alcohol or drugs or other destructive behavior is positive and suggests that she is capable of making an object connection. In a case like this the usual concern that giving advice is paternalistic and likely to promote rivalry is not relevant, at least not at this point.

In your work with her you should try to learn as much as you can about her, including her own life history and her present situation. Then you'll be in a better position to help her deal with the many issues she faces daily as a mother and as a person who is ill equipped to deal with life in general. If you think about her diagnostically, you will probably see her as someone so unprepared for motherhood that she doesn't have the ordinary resources that most of us can summon when faced with a new challenge. From that vantage point your "advice" will have a therapeutic tone rather than an autocratic one. You would then take on the dimension of being an auxiliary ego for her with the hope that treatment would allow her to develop some resources of her own.

Sometimes when a situation warrants giving a great deal of guidance to a parent, including some specific advice, it's important to tell the parent that you're doing this because something in her background didn't provide her with the kind of experience that would have allowed her to develop these ideas on her own. You can elaborate by including information you've gained that's relevant to your statement. You can convey that now that you're working together and she understands some of these basic ideas about her child, she will eventually be able to use her insights independently. Of course you have to be very careful in suggesting her eventual independence. Sometimes it may be unrealistic. In some cases it might cause the patient anxiety at the possibility of losing you when she is able to gain better judgment. And in some cases it would be an ego-supportive intervention to both suggest that there was a reason in the patient's history for the present difficulties and that with treatment this could give way to more autonomous functioning in her parenting role.

In other words, when the therapist takes on the role of auxiliary ego, it's often very helpful to tell the patient that you're doing just that. Of course you don't use that term. You transform it into something simple like, "Right now it's very hard for you to take Meg to school and say goodbye to her and leave, so you need some help from me in how to do this without the terrible upset that it's causing. But once we figure out why it's so hard, and how to make it more comfortable, you'll be able to do it without my help."

By saying this to the parent you are defining your role of auxiliary ego.

QUESTION: What do you mean by auxiliary ego?

ANSWER: It's a term that traditionally is used to describe a function of the caregiver during infancy, that of protecting the infant from being overwhelmed by stimuli (Edward et al. 1991). Mahler (1968) became particularly interested in investigating the consequences of the failure of this caregiving role; she found it could lead to the infant's being forced to develop his own resources prematurely, which in turn would skew the development of psychic structure and, most specifically, produce a false self.

In an earlier work (Siskind 1997) I expanded the use of this term to include a function of the therapist in various treatment situations in which the patient does not have the inner resources to deal with a situation that feels overwhelming. Sometimes we take on this role with children, sometimes with adult patients, and sometimes with the parents of our child patients. I see your role with Jack's mother as decidedly fitting this description of the therapist becoming an auxiliary ego.

QUESTION: That's very helpful. I think it applies to a lot of what we do and it feels good to give it a name and definition. I think that when I "Jack proofed" my office, I was doing something along those lines because not only did it make me feel less tense, but it made him feel much less scattered and overstimulated.

Right now I have a few more questions about the more ordinary, typical, generally well-functioning parent who is anxious about taking charge and who wants the therapist to prescribe bedtime, diet, number of hours in front of the TV, qualifications for baby-sitters, choice of books, emphasis on table manners, the size of a weekly allowance, when a girl should have her ears pierced, whether a boy should have his ear pierced, and when children should be allowed to go into public bathrooms by themselves, and so forth. What do you do with parents who want you to make all these decisions for them?

ANSWER: I know some parents are more "typical" and "ordinary" as you put it, not as extreme as Jack's mother, but it's a mistake to leave it at that. You still need to have a diagnostic formulation, even a fairly general one, but at least enough to particularize that parent. You have to ask yourself whether that father is asking your opinion because he really doesn't know, or is he checking out what you know and what you think? Is that mother asking you because she doesn't know or is she asking you because she's in a state of disagreement with her husband, her friend, her mother, or the child himself, and if you agree with her she'll quote you and if you disagree she'll keep it to herself and probably be angry at you. Or is this a father or a mother who's afraid of the child, afraid to make decisions, afraid of doing harm, being the object of the child's anger, and so forth. Is the fear the result of reaction formation, or is it a result of insufficient differentiation between self and child?

When you understand what you're being asked you're likely to know how to proceed. All the questions you listed are part of the normal issues that parents have to deal with all the time. Nothing in your training makes you more qualified to answer them than the public at large. So why are they asking you? They know much more about their child's need for sleep. Their pediatrician can give them advice about diet. They have their own attitudes about pierced ears, table manners, television watching, and so forth. Why are they asking you? You have to get behind these questions and explore them. That's what you're trained to do.

QUESTION: Aren't there some questions that have to do with raising children that we're more qualified to answer than the public at large?

ANSWER: Yes. There are some questions that a parent might ask us where our training has yielded areas of knowledge not available to the public at large. For instance, we might be able to help parents plan for a child's hospitalization by keeping in mind the major areas of anxiety that are most prominent as the child passes through the psychosexual phases. Also, we understand the particular developmental tasks and vulnerabilities that arise during the separation-individuation process. Based on what we know about these early stages of development, and what we know about the way the particular child in question has navigated through them, we might help parents understand how to approach such potentially traumatic events as serious illness, divorce, death, and other extreme situations.

I don't mean to imply that it's only with young children that we might have information helpful to parents. We might, for instance, be in a position to help parents decide whether their adolescent child's incomprehensible behavior might suggest that he might not be quite ready for an out-of-town college.

Potentially traumatic situations and important life decisions are not the only situations where our professional training gives us a particular slant. We have a way of thinking and assessing situations that's different from the public at large and applicable to a lot of ordinary everyday situations that face all parents in caring for their children. For instance, we can help parents think through and decide on a good time for their child to begin summer sleep-away camp. We can help parents assess the choice of a school in terms of whether their child might feel more secure in a structured versus a progressive school environment. But even in some of these areas where our knowledge is relevant to solving some of these dilemmas, we have to offer our thinking with a great deal of tact and sensitivity to the fact that the parents might have agendas that place importance on factors other than the ones we stress. We must be careful not to become judgmental if a parent is more interested in choosing a school of high status than in providing a comfortable environment for his child. This can be difficult to accept for the therapist who has worked hard and with great care and has seen the slow dawning of confidence in a frightened child who is now going to be sent to a school whose climate is not particularly kind or supportive, but rather fiercely competitive and academically elite. We have to be careful not to get into value clashes with parents, and sometimes that's a tall order.

QUESTION: So when parents of our child patients ask us to help them make some of these decisions, sometimes they mean it, and sometimes they just want us to agree with them. How do you know something like that ahead of time and not go offering a point of view they don't agree with that then causes tension between you?

ANSWER: If we're talking about parents of a child who's been in treatment with you for some time, and if you've gotten to know the parents pretty well, you would have a pretty good idea of whether their question is genuine or not. If the parents are consulting you, or if they have a child who's only been in treatment for a short time and you don't yet know them well and perhaps you don't have much of a working alliance with them, you proceed with caution and find out as much as you can about their attitudes.

The important issue here is that they are the parents and these decisions are theirs to make. The example of the frightened child whose parents send him to an academically elite school rather than one with a warmer and more supportive climate is a good example of where we as therapists might be taking a narrow view of the situation. We would want to see that child in a school that would place great emphasis on his total well-being and not have an investment in the academic area at the price of emotional comfort. But what if the parents were to feel very embarrassed at having their child in what they might consider a second-rate school? What if this devalued the child in their eyes, and made them feel that you, the child's therapist, were grooming their child to accept second best? They might begin to view treatment in a very negative light. In the long run your recommendation for a less demanding school, had they gone along with it, might have done their child more harm than had they sent him to the school of their choice, where he might have had to struggle hard and either grow to meet the challenge or fail to do so.

QUESTION: But how can you think that? If he failed to manage the tough school and then had to be placed in the less demanding school, wouldn't that be a terrible defeat, a real setback?

ANSWER: Probably, but sometimes that's the only way some parents might come to believe that their child's frailties are real. Look, we're talking about some very ticklish issues here. We work with a lot of people whose values are different from our own. We have to accept that an incompatibility of values is in some cases one of the conditions within which we do our work. Generally we can still do good work under such circumstances; we can still help children grow and develop. But in those cases where we disapprove of parental values we are in the greatest danger of having rescue fantasies about the child. You've heard me say this before, but I can't say it too often. *The therapist's rescue fantasies are one of the most serious impediments to treatment.*

I think the most important way we can share our skills and expertise with parents is by helping them think through the situations that baffle and confuse them.

QUESTION: I have another question but it's not about treatment, it's about money. Sometimes parents are very slow in paying my bill for the child's treatment. I find that a very uncomfortable situation. I hate to call them on the telephone and remind them that the bill is two or even three months overdue. What suggestions do you have about this practical aspect of child treatment?

ANSWER: I suggest that you *not* view this as a practical problem. It's not. It's a communication, perhaps an unconscious one, from the parents to you. You really should be paid every month by a certain date of your choosing. If your bill is not paid on time you should set up an appointment with the parents and discuss this failure on their part. Remember that the parents agreed to your fee when they began sending their child to you. Your bills are predictable from month to month. It's the job of these parents to budget themselves in such a way that the money for your bill is always available. When this doesn't happen you can assume that some issues are being expressed through the non-payment and these need to be addressed promptly.

QUESTION: But sometimes parents act as if all I care about is money, and get very disparaging about my asking for payment. With that kind of attitude I find that I let their bills accumulate because I dread calling them.

ANSWER: What you're describing warrants serious reflection. When something like that happens, you need to ask yourself what's going on between you and the parents. The kind of attitude you've described suggests that you're being given a role to play and you're accepting it. Can you say something about this?

QUESTION: I once treated a 6-year-old boy named Evan who lived with his mother. His parents had never married and his father lived a few hundred miles away but stayed with Evan and his mom on his "business" trips to New York City. Evan's mom behaved like an old-fashioned mistress insofar as she didn't work and was fully supported, and she seemed very satisfied with the arrangement. This father took full responsibility for supporting Evan and his mother, and that included paying my bill. He was an intimidating sort of man, harsh, judgmental, and quick to anger. Evan and his mom both admired and feared him and behaved as if his visits were a major event. Sometimes he was very late paying his bill, and in addition to being intimidated by him, I had no way of getting in touch with him except when he was visiting New York. I suspect he had another family back home. I noticed he made it a point to assure me that I did not need to know where he lived. According to him, my job was the treatment of his son. Knowing anything about Evan's parents was not my business.

I would mail my bill to the mother's address and when it went unpaid for a full month, I would write a note on the next bill pointing out that the previous month's payment was overdue. Sometimes four months would pass and I would finally get a check with a short unpleasant note such as: "As you see, I pay my bills. In the future omit your little notes about the bill being overdue. I find them offensive."

This father did not want to meet with me once Evan began his regular appointments. But it had been the father who had sought me out to begin with, and, after meeting with me twice prior to my meeting Evan, had decided that I would do as Evan's therapist.

I tried to speak to the mother about the late payment. She gave me an enigmatic smile and said that this was a man who did things his way or no way . . . she had learned this about him long ago and had accepted it as a fact of her life. Talking to him about my bill was something she could never do.

I realize as I tell you this long tale that in this situation I joined Evan and his mother in taking on a subservient role vis-à-vis this man. Although aware of my discomfort and resentment, I did not confront the situation, neither in regard to my part in it, nor in regard to this man treating me in a disrespectful manner. But I also want to say that Evan made excellent use of his treatment and by the end of the year I worked with him he was ready for termination. He was a bright and delightful child and a pleasure to work with. So despite my failure to deal effectively with the father's devaluing manner and late payments, I did eventually get paid all that was owed to me and the child left treatment with an excellent outcome.

ANSWER: This is a fascinating story. Had you called that father in and discussed his late payments in a serious manner, it's very likely he would have been unable to tolerate being questioned in any way and would have terminated Evan's treatment. As it turned out, by playing the role he assigned to you, that of being smaller and less powerful than he was, the treatment had a good outcome. However, despite the good outcome, you did suffer some unpleasantness and it would have been much better for you had you analyzed the dynamic of the interaction with this man. Then you might have done everything the same way without feeling you had been cast in a role that was demeaning. You would have understood how badly this man needed to feel big and what he did to those around him to achieve this goal. In other words, you would have transformed this situation into one where you were observing and using your knowledge in a constructive way, rather than simply reacting to your fear of him.

But I want to conclude this discussion about money by saying that it's important for us to get paid for our work in a timely manner and achieving this is more difficult in the treatment of children than in that of adults. When our adult patients are late in paying, this becomes a subject we discuss, analyze, and interpret. When parents fail to pay us we don't have the same ongoing treatment relationship with them and so we may lose some of our leverage. Unless parents have had a significant financial setback, our bill must be paid on the terms we outlined at the start of treatment. There is no reason to continue treating a child for months on end if his parents don't pay their bill. That would make you more concerned about the child's treatment than are his parents, a strange role reversal that bears close examination.

The expectation of receiving payment for our work and being regarded with respect for our professional training and competence are as much a part of our professional attitude as are the more obvious aspects of our therapeutic role: our interest, insight, curiosity, objectivity, and our capacity for reflection, tolerance for ambiguity, and ability to feel empathy.

14

Termination: Why, When, and How

QUESTION: How do we know when it's time to terminate?

ANSWER: That's one of your really broad questions. We'll have to talk back and forth a long time before we even begin to find a satisfactory way of approaching an answer.

A good way to start would be to talk about the goal of treatment. What, in your opinion, is our goal?

QUESTION: I can see how complicated this is because there are several people involved in the child's treatment and the therapist's goals for her child patient may not match those of the child's parents or those of the child. This is confusing. Whose goal are we talking about?

ANSWER: In some instances there is a convergence of goals. That's the ideal situation. But often a disparity in goals does exist. Let's begin with the therapist's goals since they are, or should be, the most objective, realistic, and comprehensive. How would you conceptualize the therapist's goals for a child's treatment?

QUESTION: It seems to me that goals should be connected to our original recommendation for treatment, which in turn was based on our understanding of the problem or condition that brought this child's parents to our office for consultation. But I don't know how to take it from there. I'm having trouble organizing this.

ANSWER: Well, let's approach it this way. Let's combine our original reason for recommending therapy with what we've subsequently observed and learned during the actual course of the child's treatment. This would include our work with his parents, or, in some situations, our inability to work with either or both of the parents.

After a thorough evaluation process we reached a working diagnosis. But then, as treatment got under way, we continually sharpened our understanding of this child whom we got to see in our office week after week. And as we got to know our young patient, we reminded ourselves that he was the child of his particular parents.

So, keeping in mind what was originally of concern in the child's development, as we got to know him well we revised and refined our understanding of him. For instance, we noted how well and quickly he was able to understand what treatment was about and how able he was to extract the most from it. Or maybe we noted how slow and painstaking the process was for him and how minute and hard won each incremental gain.

The ability to actually make use of treatment is not a piece of information we have about our patients until the process is under way, but it's a vital piece of knowledge with far-reaching implications. I'm providing it as an example of the kind of information we continuously uncover that feeds and expands and corrects our original assessment and informs our work with the child and with the parents.

QUESTION: Of course it's important to make good use of treatment, but you seem to view it as an ability, like a talent or some special attribute of the child that has great meaning.

ANSWER: That's true. Perhaps it's a combination of confident expectation and an ability to communicate, both suggesting that this child has had some good enough early experiences to allow a strong working alliance to develop. Or perhaps the child's early experiences were not so very good, but his capacity to extract was so good that he got the most out of his early caretakers and probably was able to engage other adults and children because of his ability to tune in and connect. Upon learning this about our young patient we have to factor this information into our original diagnostic assessment.

QUESTION: Some people in our profession consider the idea of diagnosis something that insurance companies and managed care corporations do to label people. They feel that these labels reduce something that's complicated and human, to a bunch of adjectives on a computer form.

ANSWER: I know there are many experienced therapists who object to such terms as *diagnosis* or *assessment*. Their objections are not restricted to the misuse of these terms by megacorporations with financial profit as their sole concern. Some therapists feel that these diagnostic terms create some sort of great divide between therapists and patients, one that places therapists in a position superior to that of patients, and allows therapists to label patients. They prefer to keep things loose and talk about understanding the patient, and using their clinical feel to direct their work. Of course, by

taking such a stand they create a different divide, not between themselves and their patients, but between themselves and those *other* therapists who believe that a working
diagnosis is an essential tool to understanding and working
with the patient in a very deep way.

Thinking diagnostically is a lot more work than relying on
intuition and clinical feel, and it doesn't exclude the visceral,
empathic, and other affective aspects of our work. On the
contrary, it integrates them into the therapist's total attitude.
After all, as I've mentioned before, understanding our responses is an important part of the information we need in
order to approach our work with the care it warrants.

QUESTION: But the therapists who scoff at diagnosis, what
do they think about something as respected as Anna
Freud's (1962) developmental profile? It's such a marvelous guide to considering every facet of psychic development and environmental circumstance. How can anyone ignore it?

ANSWER: Some people in our field respect Anna Freud's famous
profile as an important teaching tool and then set it aside as
a remnant of their years in training. That's too bad, but even
sadder is the fact that many therapists have never studied it
and might even be unaware of it.

I'm very grateful that the profile was an important part of
my training as a child therapist, and that this orientation was
further enhanced during my subsequent training as psycho-
analyst and psychoanalytic psychotherapist of adults. Two
of my teachers, Rubin and Gertrude Blanck, gave considerable attention to the profile when teaching diagnosis. They
also created a most valuable diagnostic developmental
schema (1974, 1994) that incorporated core concepts in
Anna Freud's profile, but was organized differently and went
beyond the profile by integrating new information about the
vicissitudes of very early development and its potential for

skewing further development. I've referred to this earlier (see Chapter 4, p. 39).

Now, before we get too far off course, we should return to our subject of the moment, which is considering criteria for termination. Let's return to your earlier statement, which correctly assumes that termination should have some connection to the original reason for treatment. So let's break this down into some general entities.

QUESTION: Diagnostic entities?

ANSWER: Yes. Let's begin with a more or less neurotic structure and a child who began treatment because of an intense phobia. Let's consider the phobia to be the outer manifestation of unconscious conflict. Then our goal would be to bring the conflict to conscious awareness, to reconstruct its genesis, and to work it through to the point of resolution. Such successful treatment would result in the phobia no longer being needed. That in turn would free up psychic energy that had been used to defend against (repress) the breakthrough into conscious awareness of forbidden thoughts and wishes. With this very favorable outcome the child's development would no longer be hampered by an ego overtaxed by its defensive operations and by the constriction of the phobia itself. With ego energy restored, progressive development would once again be able to resume a more normal forward course. The achievement of this major piece of analytic work would suggest that termination was the appropriate course of action. Forgive me for such a pat and abbreviated example but it does illustrate a situation where termination is clearly indicated.

If the child's treatment was prompted by difficulties in her relationships, which upon the therapist's observation seemed suggestive of narcissistic pathology, we might note the following. We might find a pattern of grandiosity, of difficulty in self-regulation, including swings between attempts at self-sufficiency and extreme dependency. We might find that this child is unaware of how her often provocative behavior infuriates those about her.

This would be a very different picture than that of the phobic child, and treatment would have to address the developmental deficits and/or arrests that had caused development to take this particular direction.

Often we find that children with this type of personality organization were raised in an ultra-permissive, seemingly indulgent environment. As we dig deeper we discover that neglect and abdication of parental function are masked by indulgence. We begin to understand that this child does not feel safe, has in fact not been provided with a safe environment. That failure is often the outcome of not being able to experience parental strength and the protection it provides, and results in a myriad of difficulties, including failure of identification with the "no"-saying parent, a critical component of self-regulation and identity formation.

With this particular type of pathology the therapist often becomes the first adult in the child's life who neither avoids nor becomes enraged by the child's narcissistic characteristics, which can take the form of grandiosity and entitlement, expressed in an imperious attitude. The therapist has the delicate task of finding a way to form an alliance with a child who either gets too close or stays too far away. These alternating moves between closeness and distance both lead to the child's repeated experiences of anxiety and discomfort. The therapist walks a fine line, often having to tactfully combine understanding with strength and availability with firmness.

The goal for a child suffering from this particular pathology would be to help her achieve greater self-regulation and a firming up of autonomy, both basic components of identity formation, and more evenly distributed cathexis of self- and object representations.

What I'm talking about amounts to profound changes in all aspects of development. Changes would have to take place in the child's object relations and ego functioning. A structural shift would have to occur involving a change in the relationship of id, ego, and superego.

With such effective treatment accomplished, the child would be more able to understand the world and her place in it, and more able to weather the vicissitudes of future development, including the adolescent passage. With development on a better track our work would be done, or at least done for now, and we could consider termination.

QUESTION: What do you mean when you say that "our work would at least be done for now"?

ANSWER: *When we consider termination we always do so while treatment is still ongoing. No matter how carefully we assess readiness for termination, the one thing we cannot gauge with certainty is how the patient is going to react to our actual absence from his life. Ideally, the relationship with the therapist continues beyond termination. Ideally, object representations of the therapist that formed during treatment acquire some level of permanence; they become part of the patient and the dialogue continues for life.*

QUESTION: I think I know what you mean. Sometimes we can see that happening as treatment progresses. I've had instances when a patient comes in and tells me how upset and perplexed she was because of a particular incident, even considered calling for an extra session, and then she imagined what I might ask or say and was able to have a dialogue with me without even having to see me. This dialogue helped her understand the real reason for her upset and how to get beyond her sense of helplessness.

ANSWER: That's a perfect example of one of those pretermina-
tion clues that usher in the termination phase. At first they
surprise us, and then we come to look for them. Your example illustrates that the work we do with our patients is
internalized. It becomes part of the patient's own psychic
repertoire for dealing with his inner life and the external
world of relationships, work, play, and all the day-to-day
events of life.

QUESTION: What would be an example of one of those pre-
termination clues from a child?

ANSWER: A child will say, "When I don't come here any more,
will you give my time to someone else?" Or something that
refers to the finite nature of the sessions. But we're jump-
ing ahead of ourselves. Let's go back to our discussion con-
necting the original reason for a child entering treatment and
termination.
I've talked about the **neurotic**[11] child whose symptom
might be a phobia. Then I went on to the **narcissistic** child
who feels either too big or too small, absolutely wonderful
or worthless, too close or too far away, but never comfortable for long, and experiences life as being lived under a
spotlight.
We also see children who because of constitutional factors, traumatic events very early in life, and/or abusive envi-
ronments, suffer from even more serious disturbances that
in turn skew their development. These children often fit

---

11. I have highlighted these diagnostic terms to emphasize that they
are not just adjectives or pejorative terms or labels. They are the names
of clusters of features that broadly describe the mental status, functioning, and general psychic state of people in general. They broadly apply to
the population at large. We all more or less fit somewhere within these
categories.

what is broadly referred to as the **borderline** condition, a diagnostic entity that probably describes the major portion of our child patient population. Unfortunately the term borderline is somewhat of a misnomer, for it implies that the child is on the border of neurosis and psychosis, when actually borderline is a diagnostic entity in its own right.

The borderline category is the most complex, the most elusive of diagnostic entities. I am not going to try to describe it because that would take us beyond the scope of this conversation which is oriented towards the broad concepts that underlie child treatment. Margaret Mahler and many others have written extensively about this, and reading recommendations will be listed at the end of this book.

Finally, at the extreme end of the diagnostic spectrum, we have even more serious conditions such as **symbiotic psychoses** and **autism**. With more seriously impaired children we need to have very realistic goals and not expect to bring about miracles. Yet we have to be equally careful not to confuse realistic with pessimistic. Some children might exhibit very extreme pathology at the beginning of treatment and yet make very substantial progress despite their diagnosis. Some children who are diagnosed as suffering from symbiotic psychosis or autism, whose treatment has been effective and continuous, are eventually able to go to regular schools, become good students, attend college, and become professionals in fields where their core disturbance does not interfere with their ability to do their work. Others, whose cognitive endowment is not as outstanding, might have talent in art or music and move in that direction. Still others might make their way in the world because of other talents, such as mechanical skills, fine dexterity, and even outstanding athletic ability.

Often we can play a substantial role in uncovering, supporting, and helping develop these children's natural abilities and areas of interest. Sometimes medication plays an important role in the treatment of psychotic children. It can be a valuable adjunct to psychotherapy by reducing anxiety and helping disorganized children focus. The problem is that medication is often provided as the sole form of treatment, and in those cases what is referred to as treatment is really management or containment with very little hope of forward progress.

QUESTION: You sound very optimistic about the prognosis for psychotic children. Isn't your point of view pretty unusual?

ANSWER: Probably. You see I've been lucky to have treated such children at a time when agencies were funded differently, when these children were seen frequently and were viewed as probably needing to be in treatment for most of their lives. So with medications carefully monitored and used only when absolutely necessary, and continuous work with them, their parents, and sometimes their siblings, many of them could find a place for themselves in the world. It took the combined effort of many people to achieve such results.

And even with enormous investment of effort, some of these children were too damaged to be eased into a developmental current that carried them to the periphery of the real world. But even among those who got there and entered some special place of safety in the world as we know it, their most serious limitation is and remains in the area of forming and maintaining close and reciprocal relationships. We as therapists are ready to do the lion's share of the work, and in our zeal to help the patient, we sometimes forget that the rest of the world lives by different standards and expectations.

With psychotic children our objective might be to help them contain their anxiety, improve their ability to regulate their moods, and increase the range of their affective states so that they can experience modulated affects and states of comfort. In order to reach this goal we would be undertaking a very long journey in which some of the most basic aspects of reality would be reviewed and discussed. I'll never forget a 4½-year-old psychotic child who threw a toy truck across my office and then asked me in full earnestness, "How truck got to there?" He alternated between primary and secondary process thinking, having a grasp of reality in some circumstances and none in others. At this young age he could already tell time perfectly but didn't know when he was hungry, whether toy animals urinated, and once, upon seeing my reflection in a mirror, he asked whether "that Mrs. Siskind in the mirror" could see him. He was a formidable teacher for me at the time.

So I repeat in this chapter on termination that in most cases these more disturbed children need ongoing treatment for most of their lives. Termination is more often precipitated by such external considerations as relocation and financial hardship. Treatment becomes the lifeline that supports the person's ability to function at his highest level. In the more fortunate cases, terminations simply create periods between stopping treatment and resuming the next round. In the sadder situations treatment stops for one reason or another and does not resume and the patient is not able to build or even hold on to his past progress without the presence of the therapist. In such cases, if there is no family to provide a holding environment, the individual can quickly sink and join the thousands of homeless people who grow as destitute in spirit as they are in the most basic worldly comforts and possessions.

QUESTION: So are you saying that the goal of treatment for all but the most impaired children is to bring them to the point where they can resume normal development, whereas the goal for the more impaired children is to provide ongoing treatment for life?

ANSWER: Yes, I am saying something like that, but even with the most disturbed children, the goal is still to bring them as close to normal development as their pathology will allow. Also, some very disturbed children can function for periods of time without treatment if they're in a good holding environment and if nothing throws them off balance. A holding environment could be a therapeutic school or a regular school that's sensitive to the special needs of that child. In adulthood an appropriate job can serve as a holding environment so long as it doesn't become stressful.

I want to say a little more about what I mean by normal development. I am talking about what happens inside the person. I am not talking about *looking* normal, I am not talking about going to school dressed in the right clothes for that time and place, carrying books and handing in homework, and being part of the band, and all those conventional outer manifestations of normality. I am talking about attaining a level of awareness of reality, an understanding of cause and effect in the animate as well as the inanimate world, of knowing that you will not disappear when you go to sleep, or be worthless if teased, or find yourself in great danger if you get the highest grade on a test.

I am referring to certain human attributes such as self-knowledge, self-awareness, empathy for others, achieving a level of organization and psychic equilibrium so that an ordinary affect like envy doesn't reach pathological proportions but rather is converted into serving ambition and achievement. I'm mixing various diagnostic categories to make my point.

Here's an example of how similar communications have differing bases. Over the years I've heard at least half a dozen patients bemoan the fact that they were B+ students when they really wanted to get A's. Were they talking about what kind of students they were, or was the B+ a metaphor for not being #1 as a person? What's a #1 person?

If we take the B+ as a metaphor about being the oedipal child rather than the rival parent, that's good material for analysis. But if the B+ represents the extension of what was once the toddler's age-appropriate belief in his grandiosity, customarily dashed by the disillusionment that followed during the rapprochement subphase, yet still active and alive in the patient's psychic organization in adulthood and still casting a grave shadow over his life, that's a matter that has to be addressed differently than the oedipal wish to be #1.

The neurotic and narcissistic patients who are successful in the eyes of the world are nonetheless suffering psychic pain. The origin of the pain for each is different and requires a different treatment approach.

I'm making the point that we really have to understand what's happening inter- and intrapsychically to a person, adult or child, before we can assess whether treatment has accomplished its purpose.

QUESTION: In the case of children, development is ongoing. Doesn't that make it more difficult to assess readiness for termination? How do we gauge whether normal development has been restored? What if a child was doing very well during his treatment and because of this we consider termination? Then he suffers a regression. Does that mean development slowed down again and whereas we had considered stopping we're now going to continue his treatment?

ANSWER: Well, it can be confusing and that's why we should do a careful assessment when we consider termination—an assessment not dissimilar to what ideally we do at the start of treatment.

QUESTION: Let's continue with the ideal situation. The parents are cooperative throughout the treatment and leave the timing of termination in our hands. We discuss termination with our child patient and it's agreed on. A stopping time is set. How do we set that time, and do we stop abruptly or do we wind down to less frequent appointments?

ANSWER: Stopping abruptly would never be advisable. It takes time to get used to the idea of stopping treatment. In our work with adults we often consider termination a phase in its own right and it could extend over months, or even a year and more. With children in psychotherapy it's more customary to set a stopping date two or three months after the termination decision has been made.

Whether to phase down frequency or stop on the set date is something that should be individually discussed. The child should have a voice in this decision. I like to set some follow-up visits after termination to check out the child's progress. Some of these appointments can be with the child and some with the parents. There are no rules here. We're not talking about termination in a vacuum, we're talking about making decisions with and about a child we know very well and about parents with whom we've had a long-standing relationship and whose child has done well enough to stop treatment. All this knowledge will guide our termination plan just as it guided all other aspects of our work with the child and his family.

I think many therapists have their preferred ways of stopping. That doesn't make one approach better than another. Just different. For instance I don't like having termination coincide with a vacation period, not mine or the child's. If we're ready to stop as summer approaches, I prefer to schedule another month or so of appointments at summer's end and see how things are. As you mentioned before, development is not steady and even. Sometimes regressions occur, particularly around termination. Mostly these are transient regressions, but still it doesn't hurt to follow up, to check things out, and not to stop at a point of separation from the usual routines, such as the long summer vacation.

QUESTION: What if you do all that and the child begins to have some of his prior difficulties?

ANSWER: Sometimes children need to come back for a while. If termination is carefully handled, this possibility would be built into the termination phase and both the child and parents would be helped to view such a possibility as a return to treatment—not as a failure, but simply as an indication that more work still needed to be done.

QUESTION: Now that we've talked about the ideal situation of the child and parents allowing the therapist to set the termination date, can we go on to the less ideal situations of capricious, or angry, or silent termination?

ANSWER: Sure, but before we do, I want to comment on the statement you just made. In considering termination the therapist makes an assessment based on what she sees developing in the treatment, what she learns from the parents about the child's life at home and at school, what she might learn from direct contact with teachers and school personnel, and what the child expresses when she raises the subject with him. So the decision to terminate is in no way unilateral. It is truly based on an assessment of all relevant information.

Now we can talk about the bane of a child therapist's life. The child is making slow and steady progress and is settling into the treatment situation when the parents suddenly decide it's time to stop. Or one of the parents decides it's time to stop and the other is for continuing and this becomes a major battle that the child is pulled into. Or the parents decide that their child seems happier and enjoying school more, so why not cut down to every other week?

Are those the type of situations you're referring to?

QUESTION: Exactly! It happens all too often. Just as the child is beginning to make progress the parents want to pull him out or impose conditions that make no sense. What do you do then?

ANSWER: You do your best. We talked earlier about parents making demands that you can't agree to. When they insist that frequency be reduced to an unacceptable level, you refuse. You might agree to it for a while as part of a tapering off process, but you don't have to accept ultimatums. You know a lot more about treatment than the parents; you're the professional and you don't accept working in a counter-productive mode.

    If they want to take their child out of treatment prematurely, you can try to reason with them, to explain the need for continuing, but if they want to stop they can do so at any time.

QUESTION: But what do you tell a child who's become very invested in his appointments and feels much more hopeful about himself, when his parents suddenly decide that he has to stop?

ANSWER: You tell him the truth. You do it tactfully. You tell your young patient that his parents have decided to stop his appointments. You wait to see what he has to say about it. You let him express his thoughts and feelings. You're still the therapist. You don't offer your opinion or discuss your feelings about it. The fact that you're ending doesn't alter your professional stance. Helping your patient deal with termination is your main concern.

    Often when these sudden terminations are imposed by the parent, the child is not as surprised as you are. He might even already know about it. Or you might learn that the same thing happened with the last therapist.

You listen to a child who is about to be whisked out of treatment with the same attention you applied to everything else in your work with him. If you do that, if you retain your professional attitude to the last moment of the last session, you might learn things that will really surprise you.

You might, for instance, learn that this incident, which to you seems a terrible affront, is something quite different to this child. This child might be so accustomed to loss that he's developed his own resources for dealing with loss and disappointment. He might tell you it was great that he could come for three months because you have much better toys than his last therapists. Or he might tell you he's glad to stop because there's an after-school program he can now join, or a TV show he can now watch. Or he might tell you his parents always spoil everything and that when he's grown up he'll come back and stay as long as he likes. Whatever he tells you will be consistent with how he deals with every other setback and disappointment.

QUESTION: So what do you do, just let him go? Just let him make up one of his stories and let him go?

ANSWER: You do the best possible job of discussing termination with his parents. You do your best to have a little time before actually having to stop. You try to part with the parents on the best possible terms so that if they become worried about their child they will be able to return without feeling embarrassed or worried that you're angry. And you do your very best to have a graceful ending with your young patient.

QUESTION: Do you give him a goodbye present?

ANSWER: Sometimes, but only if it's been discussed, if it's relevant to the treatment, and if it isn't going to draw fire from the parents.

QUESTION: And then what?

ANSWER: And then you say goodbye.

QUESTION: And that's it? All our work, all our effort, and we just give up and let children leave just as they were settling in?

ANSWER: It's very sad and very upsetting when that happens. But you must remember we are not the child's parents and we cannot keep children in treatment unless their parents agree to it. And while these impulsive terminations, which occur quite often, are unfortunate, sometimes even a few months of treatment might have provided the child with a new experience that might have some lasting value.

I'm going to give you a dramatic example of how even a few months of treatment in the hands of an inexperienced therapist might have had a deep impact on a young adolescent. In the case I'm about to describe, I was the inexperienced therapist. The setting was an agency for adolescent girls where as a beginning student I had my first field placement. For my very first interview I was assigned a 13-year-old girl, referred by her school for being disruptive in class and rude to her teachers. The guidance counselor at her school who had referred her described her as being very bright, but so angry at white people that the referral request had been for an African American therapist. Since none were available the case was assigned to me. My supervisor later confessed that she didn't expect this adolescent to ever return for a second session.

Jena was the next to oldest of nine children in what was then called a multiproblem family. They were poor, crowded, and life was chaotic. I saw Jena weekly for several months and, contrary to my supervisor's expectations, she became so invested in her treatment that she usually arrived two hours early and never missed a single session.

During my first session with Jena she didn't talk. She did communicate by gesture and I would try to understand what she was saying. For instance, she moved her hands as if typing and I asked her if she were pretending to type. We managed a dialogue of her gestures and my attempts to understand them and when I finally got the right message she would smile and nod. I learned that she wanted to learn to type and wanted me to give her a typewriter. Towards the end of the first session she danced for me. She was a terrific dancer in the popular genre.

In subsequent sessions Jena talked quite freely and told me a lot about her world. She was funny and clever and very taken with my interest in her. At first she could hardly believe that there was no hidden agenda, that I was just there to listen to her and be with her and discuss whatever was of interest to her that day. She thrived in that easy companionable situation. Sadly, I had to terminate our work when my placement came to an end, and she was to be transferred to my student replacement. It was hard for both of us to say goodbye, and I wondered whether some of the growth I had noted in her would remain. So often in our work, especially with children, we never know how they've fared in later life.

Jena presents me with an opportunity to end this book on a happy note. I accidentally saw her again ten years later; she was 23 then. It happened one day when I was observing a class at a school where I served as consultant. She was one of the newly placed student teachers and wore a tag with her name on it. If not for that I might not have recognized her. She was an adult now.

I went up to her and asked her if she recognized me. She didn't. I said my name. Still no recognition. I then named her mother and several of her siblings and described something about each of them. A look of amazement crossed her face.

"You remember all that!" she said. "How do you remember all that about me? You must have cared a lot about me to remember. Now I know who you are. That first time I came to see you I wouldn't talk but I showed you how well I could dance. I expected you to tell me to stop all that and sit down and talk. But you just let me and looked interested. After you left I tried to go to the next one they assigned me to but she was very bossy and I only went once. Oh yes, I remember you. You were the good one."

Then she turned to go. A child needed her help. But just before she left she turned and quickly said, "I'm becoming a teacher now, but in a few years I'm going back to school and then I'm going to do what you do."

I cannot know what part those few months with Jena played in her life. But it never hurts any of us to meet some-one along the way who lets us dance when we can't talk, and who can be remembered as "the good one."

Epilogue

Our conversations have taken us in many directions, most very much in keeping with our subject matter, the treatment of children, and some veering into adjacent areas. For instance, at times we've moved from what is involved in *doing* child treatment, to the experience of *being* a child therapist, and of having all the responsibility, frustrations, and pleasures of this role. We've discussed the importance of assessing and accepting all the conditions imposed by each therapeutic situation, but we've also considered that some conditions might prove too demanding for us at a given time, or at any time, and our obligation is to protect the patient and ourselves by not taking on cases that feel overwhelming to us. So in addition to discussing what the patient needs to grow and develop, we've also touched on what the therapist needs to grow, develop, and provide a growth-promoting climate. And while we've covered a lot of ground in these fourteen chapters, there are also important matters that have not been discussed.

Although our conversations have had an easy tone, we've addressed most of the basic issues of child treatment. While application of theory has been organic to all our discussions, what has not been spelled out is the content of the body of knowledge that comprises its theoretical base. The vast body of theory that shaped our therapeutic attitude and guided our clinical decisions has been present as a silent partner rather than one whose presence was highlighted. We have talked the language of psychoanalytic developmental object relations theory without defining or explaining our terms. This was a choice made by this author out of the belief that to have become deeply involved in reviewing and explaining the theory would have taken us too far afield from the intended goal of focusing on the treatment situation. Another strong reason for making this choice was that so much has been written about the theory and so much less about how to use it in our daily work.

However, the serious practitioner needs to have a solid foundation in the theory building that has spanned most of the twentieth century. Therefore I have provided a list of recommended readings that contains several classics as well as later writings representing the expansion and enrichment of basic theory and illustrating its evolution.

Some of the works, the early Freud papers for instance, have no direct bearing on the treatment of children. But they introduce a way of thinking that is decidedly relevant and that influenced all future works. You will note that most of the readings address psychoanalysis rather than psychotherapy. The reason for that is that psychoanalysis is the parent theory out of which psychotherapy grew, sometimes separating from the parent theory in useful and creative directions, and at other times moving into constructs both reductionistic and unproductive. The approach for treating children represented in this book is that of *psychoanalytic* psychotherapy. The best way to get a feel for how it grew out of its parent theory is to become familiar with the theory and technique of child analysis. With that in place, the modifications that convert psychoanalysis into psychoanalytic psychotherapy can be made without sacrificing or diluting its basic principles.

Our conversations have had the goal of applying theory to practice, of presenting what is referred to as treatment technique, which in plainer language means knowing what to do. To meet this objective I have tried to demonstrate how we transform the experience of being with a child, talking to a child, and playing with a child into the *treatment* of a child.

Appendix:
Basic Principles

The following, listed by chapter, are the basic principles that were highlighted throughout this book. Read out of context they might not have as much meaning as they did at the height of the chapter dialogues, but perhaps they will serve to jolt the memory and bring back the essence of what was discussed.

Chapter 1

- The factor of youth establishes two sets of conditions of primary importance: (1) development is ongoing, and (2) the child is dependent on his parents for basic care. These conditions are at the heart of the differences between treating a child and treating an adult.
- Our role with parents is to be their ally in helping them with their child.

Chapter 2

- We always have to be as mindful of our communications with the parents as we are of our communications with the child.
- The child's therapist has to stand equidistant to child and parents. Only when positioned that way can the therapist

be alert to all the subtle shifts of affect and behavior that inform and guide our work.

We need to understand what needs to be treated!

• When we are able to maintain our professional attitude, then no matter what develops, no matter what's tossed our way, we catch it and we make constructive use of it. We have no agenda for the content that's presented to us. Our goal is to use whatever happens during each session in a way that defines and shapes the treatment process, and, of course, builds a working alliance with child and parents.

Chapter 3

• It is essential that the therapist view a parent's voluntary appearance in the consulting room as signifying that that parent has a degree of hope that matters could change, a belief, no matter how slight, that help exists and is possible. Sometimes the therapist can do little else than represent that hope.

Chapter 4

• The objective of an evaluation is to have an understanding of the person we are treating so that our treatment plan and therapeutic interventions fit the diagnostic picture of the actual patient before us.
• The purpose of an evaluation is not only to assess strength and pathology. It's also a process of taking stock of the need for treatment, the readiness for treatment, and how to begin.
• When an evaluation pertains to a child we have to thoroughly assess the child and the parents and only then decide who the patient should be, who would most benefit from treatment at this time.
• During the evaluation process we are evaluating the need for treatment, the identity of the patient, the readiness to begin at this time, and the best way to begin.

Chapter 5

- No doubt all parents are pretty anxious about what we will have to say to them at the end of the evaluation process. They are apprehensive about what they might hear about their child, and indirectly about themselves. When we talk to them we must never forget that we are talking about their child. Being sensitive to that fact goes a long way towards organizing what we're going to say and how we're going to say it—how our findings and recommendations are going to be presented to this particular couple.

Chapter 6

- I object to the repetitive and exclusive use of action games because they do nothing to promote a shift from action to thinking, from drive discharge to formed thoughts. A young person, male or female, who has reached early or mid-adolescence and cannot express himself verbally, or be reflective, or identify how he feels, and hasn't developed the ability to think clearly and sequentially, is in trouble. This person is really not equipped to deal with the world as it is. Therapy offers the opportunity to do some developmental catching up. It shouldn't be squandered.
- Parents and therapists have some features in common. When parents have certain expectations of their children, and therapists of their patients, child and adult, and when these expectations are reasonable and well timed, they're growth-promoting. The growth they encourage is achieved by the ego-fueled action of mastery required to reach the expectations and is further enhanced by the recognition of the respect that prompted the expectation.
- The therapist and the therapeutic situation offer the child a very reliable and predictable environment. One of our most important attributes is our offering a safe climate, one in which it becomes possible to express some not-so-safe feel-

ings and thoughts. I have found that my refusal to let children take things home has been very useful in maintaining this predictable milieu. I present myself as the guardian of "an average expectable environment" (Hartmann 1939) and I do it with absolute conviction.

- What we are interested in is how to use toys and play to promote a treatment situation rather than having the playing become an after-school activity aimed at spending time in a pleasant way. What we are trying to achieve and understand is the transformation of play into therapeutic work.

Chapter 7

- For some children, being able to set the pace and tone is in itself a major departure from how they have lived their lives: not to have to rush to keep up, not to have to fit into a preset agenda, and not to have to be found wonderful . . . or disappointing, for either one is pretty awful. The therapy situation affords the child a chance to just be, and that's a new experience for many children.
- Being aware of the anxiety level of our patients, adults and children, is always of paramount importance. It's an essential barometer of the patient's moment-to-moment experience. When anxiety reaches very high intensity, the patient, of course, suffers terribly and will use any defense at his disposal to deal with his painful state. It's our job to be sensitive to fluctuations in our patients' anxiety states and not allow anxiety to reach overwhelming proportions.
- Considering the idea that *the patient is always right* forces us to broaden our field of awareness at the very times that we might most need to, at times when our own thinking might be too concrete, too subject to our own agendas. Embracing this extraordinarily simple yet complex idea helps us maintain a professional attitude.

- In the first session the therapist would like to convey that she is a useful and competent person who is there for the benefit of the child. Most children get a sense of the special nature of the relationship pretty fast.

Chapter 8

- You, the therapist, are the boss of the therapy situation, and that pertains to time, place, noise level, safety, care of equipment, and care of the people in the therapy room, the waiting room, and the entire therapy suite. Implicit in this principle is the goal of helping the child become the boss of his affects and behavior, a person who can think and talk instead of just acting out.
- It is of great importance not to confuse and lump together interventions and behaviors that might superficially look alike but are really very different in origin and purpose. For instance, being kind to a patient is not the same as overgratifying him. Kindness is a human attribute that is to varying degrees part of one's character. It hasn't been studied very much in our profession, but I can safely say that it is not to be confused with disregarding the abstinence rule (Freud 1915) and gratifying our patients' id wishes or even their demands for narcissistic enhancement. Being kind is not going to promote dependency any more than being interested and curious might.
- We cannot afford to get into power struggles with our patients, adults or children. When situations arise that might take this destructive turn we have to examine them carefully. In our work we always have to look at things a little differently than in the rest of life. When we do that, we maintain our professional attitude by engaging our "work ego," no matter what the situation, and in so doing deepen the treatment and strengthen the working alliance.

Chapter 9

- This child, like all young patients, does need your help, but he needs your help as a therapist. He does not need you to try to become a better parent than all the other adults in his life. He needs you to help him communicate in a way that has some fullness and dimension, that allows language and thinking to develop, and that enhances his sense of autonomy.
- Remember, our objective is to promote growth, and that needs to be reflected in how we think, what we say, and what we do about every matter that comes along, and of course it has to be reflected in our interventions.
- Whatever the issue, we need to know what we're doing and why. There are very few absolute rules that dictate our approach to treatment, but we do have to at least try to understand why we do what we do.
- Our goal is always to deepen the patient's treatment and further his development. What does it matter whether a patient wants to spill ink on our rug, bring a friend to his sessions, have us attend a school play or birthday party, or demand staying for two hours past the end of his appointment? These are all expressions of wishes. Our job is not to take them literally but to explore them. This applies equally whether the patient is a child or an adult.

Chapter 10

- With our adult patients, it's often hope that brings them into our consulting rooms; it's often hope that holds out the possibility that there's a way to change and grow and have a better life. I know it appears that it's pain and dissatisfaction that bring people to a therapist's office, but if you think about it, isn't it really the hope beneath that makes them pick up the phone and make that initial call? Hope is the basis for the working alliance. It's the prime motive to persist in the treatment situation.

Now with children it's a little different. They are brought to see us. It's not their decision to come. But when things go right, the therapy situation becomes a place of hope for them too. When I say things go right, all I mean is that there's a dawning awareness that this new stranger really wants to understand them.

Chapter 11

• The therapist is and always must be in charge of defining, protecting, and facilitating the therapeutic process.

Chapter 12

• We must always remember that people assign roles to us, and whatever the role, it's important to pay attention, note what's transpiring, and try to understand what's being enacted. We need to study the role we've been given, the interaction that follows, and our response to the interaction. Paying attention to how we handle the role we've been given is a good way of learning something about our patients and ourselves.

• When a therapist finds the behavior of a child, or parent, or any patient inappropriate, that's a red alert, a signal that the therapist needs to analyze his reaction. Very often we use the word "inappropriate" when our normal anticipatory system has been jolted, when something unexpected has happened. It's fine to react strongly to the unanticipated and take note. It's not so fine if we give the action that unsettled us a pejorative label and dismiss it as such. In our work, the appearance of what we might call "inappropriate" provides an opportunity for examining and deepening our diagnostic thinking. Often the appearance of unexpected behavior in our patients can serve as a catalyst to opening our ability to understand them more fully.

• Our work is very demanding. Maintaining a professional attitude all day long, no matter how we feel, how tired we are,

how difficult the patient might be, how charged the atmosphere might get, is hard work. And our work doesn't end
when we leave our offices. We think about our patients
when we're not with them. We write up session notes, some
of us go to supervision, attend ongoing case and theoretical
seminars and lectures, and keep up with our reading. To
become involved in the social life of our patients is not only
questionable on their account, it's questionable on our account. We need time for our private lives.

Chapter 13

- The expectation of receiving payment for our work and being regarded with respect for our professional training and
  competence are as much a part of our professional attitude as are the more obvious aspects of our therapeutic
  role: our interest, insight, curiosity, objectivity, and our
  capacity for reflection, tolerance for ambiguity, and ability to feel empathy.

Chapter 14

- When we consider termination we always do so while treatment is still ongoing. No matter how carefully we assess
  readiness for termination, the one thing we cannot gauge
  with certainty is how the patient is going to react to our
  actual absence from his life. Ideally, the relationship with
  the therapist continues beyond termination. Ideally, object
  representations of the therapist that formed during treatment acquire some level of permanence; they become part
  of the patient and the dialogue continues for life.

Recommendations for Further Reading

Abelin, E. (1971). The role of the father in the separation-individuation process. In *Separation-Individuation: Essays in Honor of Margaret S. Mahler*, ed. J. McDevitt and C. Settlage, pp. 229–252. New York: International Universities Press.

Anthony, E. J. (1980). The family and the psychoanalytic process. *Psychoanalytic Study of the Child* 35:3–34. New Haven: Yale University Press.

Anthony, E. J., and Benedek, T., eds. (1996). *Parenthood, Its Psychology and Psychopathology*. Northvale, NJ: Jason Aronson.

Beren, P., ed. (1998). *Narcissistic Disorders in Children and Adolescents*. Northvale, NJ: Jason Aronson.

Bernstein, I., and Glenn, J. (1988). The child and adolescent analyst's emotional reaction to his patients and their parents. *International Review of Psycho-Analysis* 15:225–241.

Brandell, J. (1992). *Countertransference in Psychotherapy with Children and Adolescents*. Northvale, NJ: Jason Aronson.

Cath, S., Gurwitt, A., and Ross, J. (1982). *Father and Child*. Boston: Little, Brown.

Chiland, C. (1982). A new look at fathers. *Psychoanalytic Study of the Child* 37:367–380. New Haven: Yale University Press.

Cohen, R., Cohler, B., and Weisman, S., eds. (1984). *Parenthood: A Psychodynamic Perspective*. New York: Guilford.

Edward, J., Ruskin, N., and Turrini, P. (1991). *Separation-Individuation: Theory and Application*. New York: Gardner.

Ekstein, R. (1966). *Children of Time and Space, of Action and Impulse: Clinical Studies on the Treatment of Severely Disturbed Children*. New York: Appleton-Century-Crofts.

Elkisch, P. (1971). Initiating separation-individuation in the simultaneous treatment of a child and his mother. In *Separation-Individuation: Essays in Honor of Margaret S. Mahler*, ed. J. McDevitt and C. Settlage, pp. 356–376. New York: International Universities Press.

Fraiberg, S. (1951). Clinical notes on the nature of transference in child analysis. *Psychoanalytic Study of the Child* 6:286–306. New York: International Universities Press.

——— (1969). Libidinal object constancy and mental representation. *Psychoanalytic Study of the Child* 24:9–47. New York: International Universities Press.

——— (1977). On the origin of human bonds. In *Every Child's Birthright: In Defense of Mothering*, pp. 37–71. New York: Bantam Books.

———, ed. (1980). *Clinical Studies in Infant Mental Health*. New York: Basic Books.

Freud, A. (1946). *The Ego and Mechanisms of Defense*. New York: International Universities Press.

——— (1965). *Normality and Pathology in Childhood*. New York: International Universities Press.

Freud, S. (1905). Three essays on the theory of sexuality. *Standard Edition* 7:130–243.

——— (1912). The dynamics of transference. *Standard Edition* 12:97–108.

——— (1912). Recommendations to physicians practising psychoanalysis. *Standard Edition* 12:109–120.

——— (1915). Further recommendations on the technique of psychoanalysis—observations on transference love. *Standard Edition* 12:157–171.

——— (1924). The dissolution of the Oedipus complex. *Standard Edition* 19:171–179.

———— (1926). Inhibition, symptoms, and anxiety. *Standard Edition* 20:75–174.

———— (1933). New introductory lectures on psychoanalysis. *Standard Edition* 22:1–182.

Furman, E. (1971). Some thoughts on reconstruction in child analysis. *Psychoanalytic Study of the Child* 26:372–385. New York: Quadrangle Books.

Galenson, E., and Roiphe, R. (1980). The preoedipal development of the boy. *Journal of the American Psychoanalytic Association* 28:805–827.

Geleerd, E., ed. (1967). *The Child Analyst at Work.* New York: International Universities Press.

Glenn, J., Sabot, L. M., and Bernstein, I. (1992). The role of parents in child analysis. In *Child Analysis and Therapy,* ed. J. Glenn, 2nd ed., pp. 393–423. Northvale, NJ: Jason Aronson.

Jacobson, E. (1964). *The Self and the Object World.* New York: International Universities Press.

Mishne, J. (1983). *Clinical Work with Children.* New York: Free Press.

Moore, B. E., and Fine, B. (1990). *Psychoanalytic Terms and Concepts.* New Haven: Yale University Press.

Neubauer, P. (1960). The one parent child and his oedipal development. *Psychoanalytic Study of the Child* 15:286–309. New York: International Universities Press.

Novick, K., and Novick, J. (1987). The essense of masochism. *Psychoanalytic Study of the Child* 42:353–384. New Haven: Yale University Press.

Parens, H. (1989). Towards a reformulation of the psychoanalytic theory of aggression. In *The Course of Life, Vol. 2: Early Childhood,* ed. S. I. Greenspan and G. H. Pollock, pp. 83–127. New York: International Universities Press.

———— (1989). Towards an epigenesis of aggression in early childhood. In *The Course of Life, Vol. 2: Early Childhood,* ed. S. I. Greenspan and G. H. Pollock, pp. 129–161. New York: International Universities Press.

———— (1990). Neurosis and prevention. In *The Neurotic Child and Adolescent*, ed. M. H. Etezady. Northvale, NJ: Jason Aronson.

Pine, F. (1976). On therapeutic change: perspective from a parent–child model. In *Psychoanalysis and Contemporary Science*, *Vol. 5*, pp. 175–208. New York: International Universities Press. Also in (1985). *Developmental Theory and Clinical Process*, pp.127–149. New Haven: Yale University Press.

Prior, S. (1996). *Object Relations in Severe Trauma: Psychotherapy of the Sexually Abused Child*. Northvale, NJ: Jason Aronson.

Reich, A. (1973). *Psychoanalytic Contributions*. New York: International Universities Press.

Roiphe, H., and Galenson, E. (1981). *Infantile Origins of Sexuality*. New York: International Universities Press.

Rosenfeld, S., and Sprince, M. (1963). An attempt to formulate the meaning of the concept of borderline. *Psychoanalytic Study of the Child* 18:603–635. New York: International Universities Press.

———— (1965). Some thoughts on the handling of borderline children. *Psychoanalytic Study of the Child* 20:495–517. New York: International Universities Press.

Sandler, J. (1987). *From Safety to Superego: Selected Papers of Joseph Sandler*. New York: Guilford.

Sandler, J., Kennedy, H., and Tyson, R. (1980). *The Technique of Child Psychoanalysis: Discussions with Anna Freud*. Cambridge: Harvard University Press.

Seinfeld, J. (1991). *The Empty Core: An Object Relations Approach to Psychotherapy of the Schizoid Personality*. Northvale, NJ: Jason Aronson.

Spitz, R. (1965). *The First Year Of Life*. New York: International Universities Press.

Tolpin, M. (1971). On the beginning of a cohesive self: an application of the concept of transmuting internalizations to the study of the transitional object and signal anxiety. *Psychoanalytic Study of the Child* 26:316–354. New York: Quadrangle Books.

Tyson, P. (1978). Transference and developmental issues in the analysis of a prelatency child. *Psychoanalytic Study of the Child* 33:213–236. New Haven: Yale University Press.

Weil, A. (1970). The basic core. *Psychoanalytic Study of the Child* 25:442–460. New York: International Universities Press.

Winnicott, D. W. (1953). Transitional objects and transitional phenomena: a study of the first not-me possession. *International Journal of Psycho-Analysis* 34(2):89–97.

——— (1960). Counter-transference. In *The Maturational Processes and the Facilitating Environment,* pp.158–165. New York: International Universities Press.

In addition to the above readings, it is highly recommended that regular browsing through the 50+ volumes of *Psychoanalytic Study of the Child* (in addition to the specific articles mentioned above and in the references) take place whenever the opportunity arises.

References

Benedek, T. (1938). Adaptation to reality in early infancy. *Psychoanalytic Quarterly* 7:200–214.

—— (1959). Parenthood as a developmental phase. *Journal of the American Psychoanalytic Association* 7:389–417.

Blanck, G., and Blanck, R. (1974). *Ego Psychology: Theory and Practice.* New York: Columbia University Press.

—— (1994). *Ego Psychology: Theory and Practice,* second ed. New York: Columbia University Press.

Edward, J., Ruskin, N., and Turrini, P. (1991). *Separation Individuation Theory and Application.* New York: Gardner.

Fliess, R. (1942). The metapsychology of the analyst. *Psychoanalytic Quarterly* 11:211–227.

Freud, A. (1962). Assessment of childhood disturbances. *Psychoanalytic Study of the Child* 17:149–158. New York: International Universities Press.

Freud, S. (1915). Further recommendations on the technique of psychoanalysis—observations on transference love. *Standard Edition* 12:157–171.

Hartmann, H. (1939). *Ego Psychology and the Problem of Adaptation.* New York: International Universities Press, 1958.

Kris, E. (1952). *Psychoanalytic Explorations in Art.* New York: International Universities Press.

Mahler, M. (1968). *On Human Symbiosis and the Vicissitudes of Individuation.* New York: International Universities Press.

Mahler, M., Pine, F., and Bergman, A. (1975). *The Psychological Birth of the Human Infant.* New York: Basic Books.

Sandler, J. (1976). Countertransference and role-responsiveness. *International Review of Psycho-Analysis* 3:43–47.

Sanville, J. (1991). *The Playground of Psychoanalytic Psychotherapy.* Hillsdale, NJ: Analytic Press.

Schwartzman, M. (1990). *The Anxious Parent.* New York: Simon & Schuster.

Sharpe, E. (1930). The analysand. In *Collected Papers on Psychoanalysis*, pp. 22–37. London: Hogarth, 1968.

Siegler, A. (1994). *What Should I Tell The Kids?* New York: Penguin.

Siskind, D. (1992). *The Child Patient and the Therapeutic Process: A Psychoanalytic, Developmental, Object Relations Approach.* Northvale, NJ: Jason Aronson.

——— (1997). *Working with Parents: Establishing the Essential Alliance in Child Psychotherapy and Consultation.* Northvale, NJ: Jason Aronson.

Spitz, R. (1959). *A Genetic Field Theory of Ego Formation.* New York: International Universities Press.

Weinstein, B. (1987). An application of developmental theory to technique: the concept of resistance-like behavior. *Clinical Social Work Journal* 15(4):349–355.

Winnicott, D. (1971). *Playing and Reality.* New York: Basic Books.

Index

ABOUT THE AUTHOR

Diana Siskind, formerly a senior staff member at the Child De-velopment Center of the Jewish Board of Family and Children's Services, has held faculty positions in the doctoral program in psychology at the City University of New York and the doctoral program at the Smith College School for Social Work. Author of *The Child Patient and the Therapeutic Process: A Psychoanalytic, Developmental, Object Relations Approach*, and *Working with Parents: Establishing the Essential Alliance in Child Psychotherapy and Consultation*, and contributor of book chapters, journal ar-ticles, and professional papers, Mrs. Siskind is currently on the faculty of the New York School for Psychoanalytic Psychotherapy and Psychoanalysis and maintains a private practice that encom-passes consultation with parents and supervision in addition to the treatment of adults and children. She is a member and Dis-tinguished Practitioner in Social Work of the National Academy of Practice.

Learning Resources
Centre